MIKE SCHMIDT
The Phillies'
Legendary Slugger

MIKE SCHMIDT
The Phillies' Legendary Slugger

ROB MAADDI

TRIUMPH
BOOKS

Library of Congress Cataloging-in-Publication Data

Maaddi, Rob.
  Mike Schmidt : the Phillies legendary slugger / Rob Maaddi.
    p. cm.
  Includes bibliographical references.
  ISBN 978-1-60078-318-0
  1. Schmidt, Mike, 1949– 2. Baseball players—United States—Biography.
  3. Philadelphia Phillies (Baseball team) I. Title.
  GV865.S36M33 2010
  796.357092—dc22
  [B]
                                                    2009042712

This book is available in quantity at special discounts for your group or organization. For further information, contact:

Triumph Books
542 South Dearborn Street
Suite 750
Chicago, Illinois 60605
(312) 939-3330
Fax (312) 663-3557
www.triumphbooks.com

Printed in U.S.A.
ISBN: 978-1-60078-318-0
Design by Patricia Frey
Title page photo courtesy of Getty Images
Insert photos courtesy of AP Images

For my father, Issa, a talented poet and author who always inspires me to achieve more; my mother, Hayat, who always believes in me; and my Jamie, who encourages me and supports me with unconditional love

"To be great is to be misunderstood."

—Ralph Waldo Emerson

Contents

Foreword

I can still see him. Settling into that batter's box. Wiggling those hips. Cocking those wrists. Taking a gulp of air so big, you wondered whether he could fit it all inside his lungs.

I can still see him. Unfurling the most picturesque swing in Phillies history. Loping around those bases without even a scintilla of style or a fleck of emotion.

I can still see him. Vacuuming up every ground ball between the third-base coach's box and King of Prussia. Never flopping. Never sprawling in the dirt. Making the art of Gold Glove defense look as effortless as the art of TV couch potatoedom.

Yes, the DVR in my brain must still be in perfect working order. I can tell because the Mike Schmidt highlight show is still playing, any old time of day or night, any old time someone brings up the subject of the greatest Phillie of them all.

I've always said somebody ought to write a book about Mike Schmidt. Maybe I even said it once to Rob Maaddi, because darned if he hasn't done it. It's the remarkable story of one of the most remarkable baseball players I ever covered.

I didn't cover all of Mike Schmidt's career in Philadelphia, only the last decade of it. But he left me with some memories, all right. He left my imaginary DVR full of them.

I can still see him. Heading for the box on a windswept day at Wrigley Field, in extra innings, with the score tied 22–22. Rocketing a game-winning home run off into the haze, bound for somewhere around the Miracle Mile. Ending the madness.

I can still see him. Standing in the on-deck circle in Montreal's Stade Olympique on the final Saturday of the 1980 season. Wondering if the Expos would be crazy enough to pitch to him in the tenth inning of a tie game. With a rookie catcher on deck and a whole season on the line. Well, they did. And Phillies history has never been the same.

I can still see him. Trotting down to first base on Opening Day 1986, after a trip to the plate that summed up exactly what the rest of his sport thought about him. A trip to the plate in which the opposing manager, a guy named Pete Rose, decided to intentionally walk him. In the *first inning* of the first game of the whole season.

I can still see him. Riding one of his hottest spring training heat waves ever. Squashing a mammoth home run at good old Al Lang Field in St. Petersburg, Florida, that almost cleared the parking lot and clanked off the Bayfront Center. Then doing the entire postgame interview about his hot streak while backing toward the clubhouse door, without any of us reporters even needing to ask a question, because he knew exactly what we'd ask.

I can still hear him, too, his voice booming across an open field in Cooperstown. Staring out at all those Philadelphians who had booed him, cheered him, loved him, hated him—and admitting their whole messy, crazy, love-hate affair was his own fault. Admitting that "If I had it to do it all over again, the only thing I would change is me."

I can still hear him. Leaning back in the dugout one afternoon, talking about how he'd love to manage someday. Describing how much easier it would be to spend every day at the ballpark, imparting wisdom, doing something that mattered, and never having that knot in his stomach he got trying to play. And me saying, "Wait a minute. You don't think you'd have that knot in your stomach if you managed a team that was 20 games under .500?" And hearing Mike Schmidt laugh as he said, "Wouldn't be my fault."

I can still hear him. Especially on that night one spring in Florida when I ran into him at dinner and asked him how his golf game was.

And chuckling for the last decade as I think about his reply: "I'm the same way in golf I was in baseball—a head case."

He was something, all right. He was cool. He was complicated. He was up. He was down. He could be a home-run machine. He could be a strikeout machine. He could be my favorite interview subject in America. He could be a guy who'd see me coming and start waving his arms to ward me off.

But all these years later, I love the guy. I loved picking his brain as much as I loved watching him play. He never lacked for an opinion. He never ran out of freeze frames for the highlight reel. Which is why that reel is still playing today.

I can still see him. Soaring through the electrified night on a magical October evening in 1980. Landing in the arms of his friend, Tug McGraw, as fireworks erupted behind them and 97 years of title-free misery melted away in that indelible instant. The photograph of that moment still hangs on many a wall in the city where it all went down. And the man floating through that sky is still one of the most memorable figures in the history of Philadelphia sports.

—Jayson Stark

Preface

I'll never forget Memorial Day 1989, and it had nothing to do with barbecues or picnics. Mike Schmidt retired that day, and I admit that hearing the news made me cry. I was 15 years old, and I loved baseball and the Philadelphia Phillies. Schmidt wasn't my favorite player; he was too good. I rooted for underdogs like George Vukovich, Bob Dernier, Len Matuszek, and John Russell. But I appreciated Schmidt for his greatness and I understood the magnitude of his retirement. It meant I would never see him play another game, and that hit me hard.

I recall listening to Schmidt's farewell speech from San Diego, seeing him choke up and then completely break down in tears at the end. I learned then that there *is* crying in baseball and that real men can be sensitive. My brother and I can still recite our favorite part of Schmidt's speech: "Eighteen years ago, I left Dayton, Ohio, with two very bad knees and a dream to become a Major League Baseball player... I thank God the dream came true." I still get goose bumps watching Schmidt's farewell on video.

Growing up in South Philly across the street from Capitolo Playground, I spent most of my summer days and nights playing baseball on one of the two fields. My father worked an overnight shift, so he spent countless hours in the park pitching batting practice to me, my brother, and our friends. The left-field fence on the Little League field was 234 feet away and very high; not quite the Green Monster, but close. By age 13, I was hitting them out. Coaches intentionally walked me in crucial spots in games, once with the bases loaded. I was the Mike Schmidt of the neighborhood. The comparison ends there.

Michael Jack Schmidt is the greatest third baseman to ever play in the major leagues. He hit 548 home runs, drove in 1,595 runs, and posted a .527 slugging percentage and a .267 batting average during his 18 seasons with the Philadelphia Phillies. Schmidt won three National League Most Valuable Player Awards, one World Series MVP Award, 10 Gold Glove Awards, and was named to the All-Star Game 12 times. His accomplishments landed him in the National Baseball Hall of Fame in 1995.

When he retired, Schmidt ranked seventh on the all-time home-run list and 17th on the RBI list. He consistently put up incredible offensive numbers in an era when baseballs weren't juiced, most ballparks weren't hitter-friendly bandboxes, pitchers still threw inside, and performance-enhancing drugs weren't a factor in the sport.

"When you put the whole package together, Schmidt could do it all," former teammate Larry Bowa said. "I rank Schmidt first because he didn't do 'the stuff.' You put steroids in Schmitty, that 30 [home runs] and 100 [RBIs] back then, with the pitching the way it was, that would multiply to 50 and 140. Every year."

Another former teammate, Pete Rose, once called Schmidt "the greatest player I ever played with." That's high praise from a guy who played with several other Hall of Famers during his career.

For all his remarkable achievements, Schmidt was never beloved in Philadelphia. He was criticized, booed, and underappreciated. Schmidt was perceived as having a nonchalant attitude toward the game and the fans, when in reality, he cared too much. He played the game with ease because he had so much natural talent.

Mike Schmidt was simply the best.

CHAPTER **1**

Child Prodigy

"I didn't know who Schmidt was, but I saw this little kid with a terrific arm catching the ball behind his back, and I said, "That has to be Schmidt.""

—Jack Fenner

"Dayton, Ohio 1963." The commercial opens with that caption. There are a bunch of Little Leaguers playing baseball in a park. A young boy approaches a smaller kid who is taking a big gulp from a carton of milk. "Hey Schmidt, you're up," the boy says. The wavy-haired kid puts down his milk and makes his way toward the plate. Seeing this, the catcher stands up, motions to his fielders, and screams, "He's up!" The pitcher turns to his fielders, waves his arm, and yells, "Back up!" The outfielders scurry back toward the wall. One tells the other, "That kid's up." Beyond the outfield fence sits a colonial-style house. A woman opens a window on the second floor and shouts a warning to the neighborhood: "Move your cars! He's up!" Tires screech as several cars whiz out of their driveways and pull away safely down the street.

The little slugger digs in and chokes up a few inches on his bat. The pitcher peers in for the sign from the catcher and confidently says, "Okay, Schmidt, this is where your lucky streak ends." He winds up and delivers a fastball right down the middle. The batter takes a mighty swing. The crack of the bat meeting the ball is thunderous. Suddenly, the image on the screen turns into an older Mike Schmidt smacking a home run for the Philadelphia Phillies. The narrator tells us, "Mike Schmidt drank his milk and he still does."

Many television commercials stretch credulity, but this milk advertisement filmed in the late 1980s was no Hollywood fabrication. Mike Schmidt was a dangerous hitter from the first time he whacked a Wiffle ball in his backyard on Pinecrest Road in Dayton. Even when Schmidt was a young boy, outfielders backed up when he came to the plate. The little guy with the freckled face and red hair had a well-deserved reputation as a hitter and all-around fine player before he was old enough to play Little League baseball.

When coaches held a draft for the 1958 North Riverdale Little League season, Schmidt was chosen with the third overall pick to play in the major league division for 11- and 12-year-olds. At the time, young Michael was only eight.

Jack Fenner was a coach and founder of the league. He fell in love with Schmidt the first time he saw him play. "We were having tryouts for the 1958 season," Fenner recalled. "Boys 12 and under in one place and the 10-and-unders in another. They were doing certain drills. I didn't know who Schmidt was, but I saw this little kid with a terrific arm catching the ball behind his back, and I said, 'That has to be Schmidt.'"

Fenner was in his second year in the league. Rules permitted coaches to select players in the draft through a bidding process based on a point system. Each coach was allotted a certain amount of points before the draft. Fenner wanted Schmidt on his team so badly he was willing to spend as many points as it would take to get him.

"I knew, with the boys I had coming back, that if I could get Schmidt I'd be set for five years," Fenner said. "I knew Mike would go pretty high, and there were two other coaches who had more bidding points than I had going in. I think a 12-year-old was the first kid drafted. Then another team drafted an 11-year-old, and that's when I got Mike. I was going to get Mike if it cost me all my points. I had about 50,000 to 55,000 points in all, and I think Mike cost me about 35,000 of them."

Schmidt skipped right past T-ball and the usual three years in the minor league division; he went right to the majors to play against boys four years older than he was.

"Playing with older guys helped me, and I don't think I gave that a second thought," Schmidt said later. "I had been playing with the same guys down at the local playground. We had pickup games, softball games, touch football, hardball. They were all three, four years older than me. I always had to play with older kids in order to feel competitive, to have the competition I needed."

Fenner was already known as a strict disciplinarian after just one season as a coach in the league. Other kids had warned Schmidt that Fenner was "a mean guy." But Schmidt had no problem playing for the tough coach. "I can't say enough about Mr. Fenner," he said. "I still remember his bunt signal. If he had his pipe upside down, we're supposed to bunt. One day we had a little light mist and he turned his pipe upside down to keep the rain out, and about six guys bunted in a row."

Schmidt was a switch-hitting shortstop, third baseman, catcher, and pitcher. He pitched three no-hitters when he was 10 and had a .737 batting average that season. He struck out 17 of 18 batters in one game against 11- and 12-year-olds. When he was 12, Schmidt hit 18 homers in a 12-game season. He was a superstar in the league and newspapers around town always wrote stories about him. With Schmidt leading the way, Fenner won four North Riverdale Little League championships in five years, compiling a 56–4 record in league play.

"He was born an athlete. That's what he always was. Always," said Schmidt's sister Sally, who was four years younger.

Michael Jack Schmidt was born on September 27, 1949, in Dayton, Ohio, a small river town located in the southwestern part of the state. His father Jack worked for a linen supply company; his mother Lois worked at a swimming pool that her family owned. Mike got his athletic genes from his parents. Jack was a three-sport letterman and was voted most athletic in high school; he later became a tournament golfer. Lois was an accomplished swimmer and once had a 156 average in bowling.

Before he turned four years old, Mike was already swinging a regulation Little League bat at the Wiffle balls his grandmother, Viola Schmidt, tossed him in the backyard. Mike was a tough little kid, too. He once got zapped by 4,000 volts of electricity while climbing a tree in his yard. Mike crashed down from the branch he was standing on and slammed into the ground. Lucky to be alive, he was rushed to the hospital and for years wore the scars from the injury on the palm of his right hand (where the electricity entered) and on his right shin (where it exited his body).

Jack Schmidt did not believe in spoiling his children. When Mike was five, his father left his job at the linen supply company to operate Jack's Drive-In, a fast-food restaurant located next to Lois' family's swimming pool, the Phillips Aquatic Club. It was not long before Mike and Sally took summer jobs at the restaurant and pool. Mike held several different jobs over the years. In his first, he earned 50¢ an hour cleaning the place with a broom and dustpan. The next year he worked as a locker boy at his grandfather's pool. He worked the counter at the restaurant, where he took orders from customers, dipped ice cream, and ran the soda fountain. But the most glamorous job for Mike was being a lifeguard at the swimming pool, so he worked hard to pass all the required lifesaving courses and got the gig.

Working odd jobs allowed Mike to make extra money aside from his allowance. He spent most of his money on model airplanes and trains. But playing sports was his passion; Mike loved to play baseball, football, and basketball, and dreamed of one day becoming a professional athlete.

* * *

Tony Lucadello had his eye on Schmidt from the time Mike was a sophomore in high school. But the short, Italian baseball scout never let on to others in his profession how much he coveted the talented young ballplayer for fear they would become more interested and recommend him to their teams.

"The less other scouts know about how I feel toward a ballplayer, the better chance I have of getting him," Lucadello once said.

Lucadello usually wore a tie and snap-brim hat and took unusual measures to make sure he was never noticed by the player he was watching. He sometimes hid in trees or behind bushes to see Mike Schmidt play baseball at Dayton Fairview High School. He once sat in the back of a station wagon to avoid getting noticed. He even befriended a janitor at the high school who allowed him to watch games from the roof of a building that overlooked the playing field.

When Lucadello signed Schmidt to his first professional contract with the Philadelphia Phillies in June 1971, the old-timer called it "the culmination of six years of some of the most intense scouting I ever had to do. Secrecy was the main thing."

Born in Thurber, Texas, to first-generation Italian immigrants, Lucadello grew up on the tough streets on Chicago's South Side. He fell in love with baseball at an early age and dreamed of getting a chance to play in the big leagues. But Lucadello lacked the talent and the size—he was just 5'5"—to make it to the majors. He spent a few years playing shortstop and managing in the St. Louis Cardinals' minor league system at the Class D level in the late 1930s. Lucadello played hard, lived a clean life, and knew the fundamentals inside and out. After a shoulder injury ended his not-so-promising playing career, Lucadello moved on beyond baseball.

He took a factory job in Illinois, met his wife, and settled down. But baseball was in his blood. He could not survive without it. Lucadello returned to the game as a part-time scout for the Chicago Cubs in 1942. He also ran tryout camps and assembled teams to compete with some of the most talented players in the Midwest. Lucadello brought two pitchers to Cubs owner Philip K. Wrigley and Cubs manager Charles Grimm in two years, and Wrigley was so impressed watching the second pitcher, Bob Rush, throw at a tryout camp that he instructed Grimm to hire Lucadello.

"Before you sign this pitcher here, if you want him that bad, you better sign that young man right there," Wrigley said, pointing to Lucadello. "This young man was born to be a scout."

Lucadello was unlike most scouts, and it was not because of his appearance (he looked more like a jockey). While most scouts usually sit behind home plate to watch a game, Lucadello preferred moving around so he could get a view of the faces of both the batter and the pitcher. He also liked to get a better read on a player's arm strength and footwork by watching from the base lines. Lucadello worked 14 years with the Cubs before joining the Phillies in 1957. He covered the Midwestern states of Illinois, Ohio, and Kentucky for the Phillies until 1989 when he committed suicide at age 76 on a baseball field in Fostoria, Ohio. The field was later named after him.

Schmidt was Lucadello's prized find, though he may have never noticed him without a major assist from Ed French, one of his part-time helpers. French first saw Schmidt play in the spring of 1965. He immediately called Lucadello with a tip about this special prospect.

"I went to check him out, and right away I could see he was an excellent athlete and an above-average prospect," Lucadello said. "Sometimes he would do things that would amaze me. Other times he would make errors or look just terrible at the plate. This gave me an edge right away, see, because other scouts, they'd see him and they'd pick at all those flaws. But I sensed that Mike Schmidt would be a late bloomer."

The introduction of the amateur draft changed Lucadello's approach, and he had to devise a strategy to scout Schmidt while keeping a low profile. During Schmidt's high school years, Lucadello said he never once contacted him, his parents, his coach, or anyone else close to him. But Schmidt was not an all-city or an all-state player in high school and he was not considered a big-time prospect. He was known more for his defensive skills at shortstop than for his hitting.

"Mike was a power hitter who struck out a lot," said Dave Palsgrove, one of Schmidt's high school baseball coaches. "He'd hit it a mile or strike out. He had a good, strong arm and he could field. The thing you worried about was, could he hit the ball enough? There's no question though, Mike was determined. He had operations on both knees, and that held him back for a while. But he wanted to excel at the game and he did."

Schmidt also played football, and basketball was his best sport in high school. He made the freshman football team and then earned a spot as the only sophomore on the varsity squad a year later. Schmidt played safety and returned punts. In a game against Colonel White High, Schmidt fielded a punt and turned upfield. He twisted to avoid a tackler, but his left cleat got stuck in the turf and he crumpled to the ground. After limping to the sideline, Schmidt's knee swelled up so much his football pants had to be cut off. Surgeons repaired the torn ligaments the next morning and Schmidt was back playing basketball before his knee had completely healed.

By the time his junior year arrived, Schmidt wanted to play football again. His mother advised against it, but his father figured they should not hold him back. Schmidt earned a starting spot at quarterback and also played regularly on defense. After intercepting a pass during a game against Belmont High, Schmidt heard something tear in his right knee. He played through it until surgeons repaired the damage early in his senior year.

The second operation ended Schmidt's football and basketball careers, and left his baseball hopes in serious jeopardy. Recruiters considered him damaged goods. But Schmidt was a hard worker on the field and was fiercely dedicated. He stayed late after practice and took extra hitting at the batting cages on his own. But all that work did not reflect in his statistics his senior season: he batted only .179 with one home run, though it came in an important spot. Schmidt connected in the thirteenth inning of a game against Meadowdale High School that won the city championship for Fairview.

"He hit one out of sight batting left-handed," said Bob Galvin, who was Schmidt's coach that season. "He hit that booger out to the left-center-field area. There was no fence there, but there was an asphalt road, and the ball hit that road and started rolling right down the road. Nobody even bothered to get it. We never saw it again. Last time I saw it, it was rolling toward the Tennessee border."

Despite his heroic finish, it was no surprise that Schmidt did not draw any serious interest from big colleges and he did not receive any scholarship offers. Schmidt figured he had to plan for a life outside of baseball.

"I was about the fourth- or fifth-best baseball player in high school—a .250 hitter, and if you don't hit .400 in high school, nobody knows you're alive," Schmidt said. "I was always the kid with potential, but even that potential was jeopardized by a couple major injuries in high school. I also was a late bloomer when it came to confidence and aggressiveness. I don't think I was really willing to fight for myself until I got to college. Not that I wasn't cocky in high school about my athletic ability. I knew I had as much talent for sports as anyone; I felt that whatever the season, I'd be the best athlete. But there were other players who had all the physical qualities I had and something else besides: they were meaner than I was, tougher mentally.

"That kind of toughness has much to do with upbringing and environment. When you come from the type of background I did—not having to fight for anything, or get out and scuffle—you grow up differently from those kids raised in a rougher environment. In my experience, when those two types confront each other on an athletic field, the kid with the rougher background has the upper hand. That lack of toughness, along with the injuries, curtailed whatever hopes I had of becoming a college athlete, let alone a major league baseball player. As it turned out, I went off to Ohio University with a T-square and a portfolio to study architecture, but I didn't give up on baseball."

Schmidt enjoyed a drafting course he took during his senior year in high school. That led to his interest in architecture. "Using a T-square and a triangle to create working drawings lit my fire," he said. Schmidt chose to go to Ohio University because it has a strong reputation for having an excellent architecture program. It helped that OU also had a solid baseball team with a well-respected coach named Bob Wren. The Bobcats coach heard about Schmidt from a friend, and he had recruited one of Schmidt's high school teammates, catcher Ron Neff. Wren invited Schmidt to try out for the freshman team as a walk-on and he earned a roster spot. Tony Lucadello and Wren were friends, and their relationship helped the scout keep close tabs on the youngster.

Schmidt also tried out for the freshman basketball team and ended up becoming the starting guard. He had a tough time with the rigorous conditioning drills, but coaches overlooked his deficiencies because he was an excellent passer and outstanding shooter. Schmidt eventually was dropped from the team after an insurance examiner informed school officials that his medical history made him too much of a risk. He took it hard, but was determined to rebuild those gimpy knees so he could play baseball. Schmidt reported to a trainer who developed a program that helped him increase the strength in his legs and allowed him to play baseball.

Schmidt struggled his first season, hitting just .260 with only one home run. He also made a ton of errors playing shortstop. Still, it did not discourage Lucadello.

"The hardest thing about scouting is projecting if a player's mind is ahead of his body or if his body is ahead of his mind, and guessing when they'll get together," Lucadello said. "With Mike, his mind was ahead of his body, which I knew from watching his face and from talking with his coach."

When Schmidt returned home for the summer, his confidence was shot. "My potential career was hanging in the balance. I could have gone either way," he said. Schmidt's father thought the best way for his son to regain his confidence was to play in Dayton's National Amateur Baseball Federation Summer League, one of the strongest amateur organizations in the nation. Jack Schmidt went to a game to watch the defending national champions, the Parkmoor Restaurant Team, and asked coach Ted Mills if there was room for his son on the roster. Mills had seen Schmidt play in high school and thought the kid was more interested in other sports.

"I was totally unimpressed with his play in the field and felt that he just wasn't interested," Mills said. "There was something about his attitude."

Mills told Schmidt's father the name of another team he could try, but Mike and his dad returned before Parkmoor had completed the first game of a doubleheader. Jack Schmidt asked Mills to reconsider. Mills told him to stick around and he would let Mike play in the second game. Schmidt was at every practice from then on. He finally started making solid contact with the ball, and one day he hit four long shots that really impressed the coach.

"I said right then, 'I don't know what happened to this kid, but he really wants to play,'" Mills said.

Schmidt earned a roster spot when Parkmoor's starting left fielder, Jim Hairston, was drafted by the St. Louis Cardinals. Schmidt became the team's regular shortstop and worked his way up the lineup from the eighth spot to third in the batting order.

"I had an excellent team returning, and I turned Schmidt down a number of times," Mills said. "Schmidt, 18 at the time, filtered his way to shortstop and became our regular at a position where I normally look for more experience. He was the youngest shortstop I ever had."

Schmidt played in two amateur leagues that summer and led both in home runs. "I had never seen a player improve so fast in so short a time," said Mills, who called Wren to inform him of Schmidt's great summer. Mills also wrote a letter to the California Angels, for whom he was a consulting scout.

A successful summer was exactly what Schmidt needed to lift his confidence at a time when it was nearly destroyed. "Ted Mills came along at a time when I desperately needed somebody to help me," Schmidt said. "Had not Ted given me an opportunity to play that summer, I probably would never have made it."

Schmidt returned to school with his mind set on becoming a major leaguer. "No one at Ohio University could believe the amazing improvement in his baseball in just a summer," said his roommate Bill Toadvine. "In the fall upon his return, Mike started talking about playing in the big leagues and how he was going to hit a home run off Bob Gibson, the great Cardinal pitcher."

Wren was able to get Schmidt a one-third scholarship before his sophomore season. The coach told Schmidt to abandon his switch-hitting and concentrate on batting strictly from the right side. Schmidt was concerned he would strike out too much from the right side because he had trouble with the curveball, but Wren assured him he would stick with him even if he struggled.

Schmidt got a big break that year when the Bobcats' starting shortstop, Rich McKinney, was drafted by the Chicago White Sox. That opened up the position for him, and Schmidt made sure he was ready to be the starter by working on his swing all winter. He spent countless hours hitting balls off a batting tee in the field house with a weighted bat and doing it all from the right side.

With his new, smooth swing, Schmidt batted .312 with seven home runs and 24 RBIs in 30 games as a sophomore, helping OU win the first of three straight Mid-American Conference championships. Schmidt hit .333 with 10 home runs and 39 RBIs his junior season and was named to the All-America team. The Bobcats qualified for the College World Series and defeated top-ranked Southern California in the first round before losing to Florida State and Texas.

Both summers, Schmidt went to play for Peoria in the Central Illinois Collegiate League. The team was comprised of All-Americans and other top college players from across the country. Many of the players had summer jobs in Peoria, but their top priority was baseball and trying to attract the attention of scouts.

Schmidt worked in a foundry, a factory that produces metal castings. "I vividly remember that job," he said. "I had to wear special shoes and a hard hat. I came out of there black. By noon, I'd be black with soot, like I came out of a cave. After a day's work, you had to take yourself a nap in order to have any energy to play ball that night."

Schmidt disliked the job so much that he phoned his parents one day and asked to come home. They talked him into staying, and he worked only half-days afterward so he would be fresh to play at night.

Playing in a competitive league only helped Schmidt continue to improve. He batted .331 with 10 home runs and 35 RBIs in his senior season and earned All-America honors for the second straight year. He finished his college career with a school-record 27 home runs.

"Mike was one of the most dedicated players I've ever had," Wren said. "He worked hard to strengthen those knees and developed great upper body strength in the process. Scouts kept coming to me and asking about him, always mentioning the knees, and I pointed out that he never missed a game with us and could do anything physically required of him."

Lucadello and Angels scout Carl Ackerman were the two scouts most interested in Schmidt. Others had their doubts.

"No one else ever did care for him in high school that much," said Red Brown, a former scout for the St. Louis Cardinals and New York Yankees. "I know he didn't really hit for me when I saw him. And he's always had those bad knees. But hey, Tony got 50 players to the big leagues, so he must have seen something."

Rich Sander, a recommending scout who worked under Lucadello, disagreed with his boss' assessment of Schmidt, though he did not argue his view too strongly.

"He didn't have a hole in his swing, but he had that long looping swing that didn't make that much contact," Sander said. "That's what you remember, his power. I'm sure that's what Tony liked. He'd hit balls through trees, and they wouldn't even slow down. But he struck out a lot, even then. And his average wasn't all that great. Tony had his mind made up. And when he did, you weren't going to change it. I know he saw Mike a ton more times than I did."

Lucadello made sure Phillies farm director Paul Owens went to Ohio to see Schmidt play in person. The trip was worth it. "That day I hit a long home run, stole a base, went from first to third on a single, and threw a runner out at first from deep in the hole at short," Schmidt said. "In other words, I did about everything a prospect could do—except maybe pitch a couple shutout innings in relief—at exactly the right time in front of the right audience."

Owens projected Schmidt as a third baseman because his upper body strength and power were more suited for that position. Besides, the Phillies already had a young shortstop in Larry Bowa.

"It's a funny thing, how sometimes you're so sure of some things," Owens said. "From the day I saw him play the first time, I knew. My first reaction was, if we're lucky to get him, there's my next third baseman."

Hoping to scare off other scouts, Lucadello often reminded them of Schmidt's bad knees in the months leading up to the amateur draft of June 1971. The Phillies held the sixth overall pick in the first round, and despite Lucadello lobbying Owens to select Schmidt, they chose pitcher Roy Thomas instead. Knowing the Angels were interested in his prized prospect at No. 13, Lucadello thought Schmidt would end up there. "My heart just sank," he said.

But the Angels drafted pitcher Frank Tanana, and when the Phillies' turn came up in the second round, Schmidt was still on the board and Philadelphia grabbed him. Right before Schmidt was chosen, the Kansas City Royals drafted third baseman George Brett. He turned out to be a 13-time All-Star and was a first-ballot Hall of Famer. Other notable players selected ahead of Schmidt include Hall of Fame outfielder Jim Rice (No. 15) and pitcher Rick Rhoden (No. 20).

Lucadello visited Schmidt and his parents a few days after the draft and offered him a $25,000 contract. Jack Schmidt sent Lucadello away without a signature, telling him that he'd better increase the offer. On June 11, Lucadello met with the Schmidt family at a Holiday Inn in North Dayton. They agreed on a $32,500 deal with incentive bonuses that could total another $7,500. An extra perk was an invitation to go to Philadelphia and work out with the Phillies during a weekend series against the San Francisco Giants.

Schmidt could not wait to sign his contract and finally realize his childhood dream. He spent part of his signing bonus on a bright-yellow 1971 Corvette Sting Ray fastback, which cost a little under $10,000. Money was not going to be an issue for Schmidt anymore.

Schmidt rooted for the Cincinnati Reds as kid, but now he would be wearing a different shade of red for the Phillies. Schmidt and his father flew to Philadelphia for his big weekend at the brand-new Veterans Stadium. When Schmidt arrived at the ballpark, he was in awe. He entered the clubhouse and met with Phillies manager Frank Lucchesi in his office. Equipment manager Kenny Bush then gave Schmidt his own uniform. He clutched it the way a child hangs onto his present on Christmas morning. Bush also gave Schmidt a couple pairs of cleats, one for artificial turf and one for grass.

"It was so surreal, as if I were in a dream," Schmidt said. "I was shaking like a leaf. This wasn't like any locker room I had ever envisioned, much less seen."

The first player Schmidt met was the one whose job he would end up taking: John Vukovich. The two became close friends over the years. Schmidt walked around the locker room and met a few more people before heading out to the field for batting practice.

Schmidt's hitting group consisted of Joe Lis, Oscar Gamble, Byron Browne, and Roger Freed, who wore No. 20. Dallas Green, who was the assistant director of the Phillies' minor league system at the time, threw batting practice to Schmidt.

"He was a great athlete, had a wonderful build, just a hell of an athlete," Green recalled. "Pope [Paul Owens] did a helluva job bringing him in. With his size and power, he wasn't a true shortstop, but athletically, he could've played it and played it well."

Schmidt hit three balls into the seats in left field and then grabbed his glove to take infield practice with Bowa, who was in his second season as the team's starting shortstop. A feisty player who worked hard to make it to the majors, Bowa was not thrilled the Phillies had drafted someone who played his position.

"I didn't worry about him taking my job, but I thought at the worst they might ask me to play second," Bowa said. "I just kept working hard. I didn't need to be pushed."

After the weekend series against the Giants, the Phillies went to Reading for an exhibition game against their Double-A affiliate. Guess who went along for the ride? Schmidt not only made the trip, but he was the starting shortstop for the Phillies because Bowa was ill. Schmidt made the most of his opportunity. He hit a game-winning home run off Mike Fremuth to give the Phillies a 4–3 victory. His performance that weekend was so impressive that management scrapped its original plans to send him to Class A ball and kept him at Reading.

Schmidt quickly realized that playing in the minor leagues lacked the luxuries he enjoyed in his debut weekend with the Phillies. He joined his Reading teammates for the first time after a road game in Elmira, New York. The clubhouse was smaller than the one at Ohio University, and players showered in shifts in a "rundown shack" of a clubhouse below the stands at the stadium.

"It was at this time I realized that I'd led a very sheltered life up until then," Schmidt said. "I was on my own now, in a world where guys had been scratching for several years to get to this level. And I was scared."

Schmidt's first year in the minors was tough. He did not get along with many of his teammates aside from catcher Bob Boone, who was moved from third base to make room for Schmidt. Most of the guys on the team looked at Schmidt as a cocky kid, a high draft pick who had been handed a job without earning it.

Pat Bayless, who was a highly regarded pitcher at one time, was Schmidt's roommate in Reading. They lived in a small, musty room in a shabby downtown hotel. Bayless moved quickly through the minor league chain his first three years until a disappointing season at Triple-A Eugene led to his demotion. He returned to Reading and became one of Schmidt's best friends on the team. Bayless had a drug problem, however, and he was released before the end of the season.

Meanwhile, Schmidt had his own problems. Adjusting to professional pitchers was tougher than he expected. He played shortstop and third base and batted mostly out of the eighth spot in the lineup. His final statistics were hardly impressive: a .211 batting average with eight home runs and 31 RBIs in 74 games. Hitting the slider was his biggest problem.

Schmidt's struggles led to Lucadello taking some heat from Phillies management after the season. "This kid's a late bloomer," he insisted. "I've seen it before. He'll develop."

Schmidt played in the Instructional League in the fall and was ticketed for Triple A in 1972, though his brief stint at Reading did not merit a promotion. "I sure didn't deserve to go to Triple A based on my half season in Double A," Schmidt said.

Granny Hamner, who played for the Phillies' pennant-winning "Whiz Kids" team in 1950, thought otherwise. Hamner, a roving minor league instructor for Philadelphia, put more stock in Schmidt's eight homers than his 66 strikeouts. He convinced the higher-ups to move Schmidt up a level to play for Eugene manager Andy Seminick, who was the catcher on that 1950 club that lost to the New York Yankees in the World Series.

When Schmidt reported to Eugene in the spring, John Vukovich was moved to second base to accommodate Schmidt, and both players struggled early in the season. Owens considered sending Schmidt back to Reading, but Seminick wanted to keep him. Seminick then decided that moving Schmidt to second base might improve his hitting because he would concentrate more on the defensive adjustment. It worked.

"Moving to second took the pressure off my hitting because, for once, I totally stopped thinking about what to do at the plate. I focused 100 percent on playing second," Schmidt said. "So naturally I started hitting like a fool, using right field, and hitting the breaking ball."

Schmidt played well defensively at second base and was even better at the plate. He finished with a .291 average, 26 home runs, and 91 RBIs, earning a September call-up to the Phillies. But Schmidt's major league debut was put on hold after he injured his knee while turning a double play late in Eugene's season. While Eugene advanced to the Pacific Coast

League playoffs, Schmidt prepared for another knee operation. He joined the Phillies, put on the uniform, and hobbled around the clubhouse on crutches.

Schmidt's surgery was scheduled for the first week of September at Temple University Hospital. It was to be performed by Dr. John R. Moore, the chairman of orthopedic surgery. When Moore entered Schmidt's room for a pre-operation conference, he had other plans. After examining the X-rays, Moore led Schmidt into the hallway. Schmidt was dressed in a hospital gown and was a little groggy from his medication, but he followed the doctor's orders. Moore instructed Schmidt to take a three-point stance as if he were a football player, and told him to fire out and run down the hallway. Schmidt did it to the surgeon's satisfaction. Moore was convinced Schmidt's knee would heal without surgery, so he told him to return to the Phillies and prescribed a rehabilitation program instead.

Within a week, Schmidt was ready to play in his first game with the Philadelphia Phillies.

CHAPTER

2

It's Showtime

"Watching him his first year in the big leagues, you knew he was going to be something special even though he hit under .200. He hit some balls that I've never seen guys hit before."

—Larry Bowa

The date was September 12, 1972. The Philadelphia Phillies were finishing another dismal season, their fifth straight year with a losing record. They had 49 wins and 87 losses and were dead last in the National League East entering a game against the New York Mets. It was an otherwise insignificant game that would bring the team one game closer to the end of the season, one game closer toward its inevitable vacation.

For Mike Schmidt, it was a day he had looked forward to his entire life. From the days as a youngster in Dayton when he was hitting his grandmother's pitches in the backyard to his struggles on the diamond in high school to his brief stint in the minors, Schmidt had dreamed of playing in the big leagues. Now the moment had arrived. He was ready to start a career that eventually would land him in the National Baseball Hall of Fame.

A couple months before Schmidt made his major league debut, Paul Owens moved from the front office to the dugout. Owens was the team's farm director when he replaced John Quinn as the general manager in June. Five weeks later, he fired Frank Lucchesi and took over as the manager because he wanted to get a closer look at the young players so he could make better individual evaluations at the end of the season.

"You guys got the team where it's at," Owens told the veterans after getting the job. "And now I'm gonna play some of the younger guys. I want you pulling for 'em, rooting for 'em."

Overall, the Phillies were a very young team. Only one regular position player, catcher John Bateman, was over 30 years old. Larry Bowa, 26, was in his third season as the team's shortstop. He batted .250 and led the league with 13 triples. Greg Luzinski, 21, was in his first full season in the majors. He hit .281 with 18 home runs and 68 RBIs. Center fielder Willie Montanez, 24, was suffering through a sophomore slump after hitting 30 home runs and driving in 99 runs as a rookie in 1971. He hit .247 with 13 homers and 64 RBIs.

Tommy Hutton played first base, Denny Doyle was the second baseman, Don Money played third, and Roger Freed got a majority of the starts in right field. They were all in their midtwenties. Youngsters Oscar Gamble and Mike Anderson also split time with Freed in right.

Steve Carlton, 27, was the ace of a pitching staff that did not have another pitcher who won more than seven games. In his first season after joining the Phillies in a trade from the St. Louis Cardinals, Carlton went 27–10 with a 1.97 ERA to win the first of his four National League Cy Young Awards.

The veterans, particularly Bowa, looked at Schmidt and other rookies like Bob Boone and Craig Robinson with icy stares. The youngsters were viewed as competition for the veterans' jobs. Schmidt was not in the starting lineup the night he made his debut against the Mets, but in the top of the second inning, Owens sent Schmidt out to replace Money at third base.

Wearing No. 22, Schmidt came to the plate for the first time leading off the bottom of the third against Mets right-hander Jim McAndrew and promptly struck out. Two innings later, Schmidt reached on an infield single to deep short for his first hit. He struck out in the seventh and drew a walk his last time up to finish 1-for-3 in his major league debut.

Schmidt got his first start the next night against tough Mets left-hander Jon Matlack. Batting seventh, Schmidt was hitless in four at-bats and had two strikeouts and one walk. After sitting out a game, Schmidt was back in the lineup in the sixth spot in the batting order against the Montreal Expos on September 16.

The Phillies trailed 1–0 when Schmidt came up to face left-hander Balor Moore in the bottom of the seventh inning. There were two outs and two runners on. The Expos intentionally walked Roger Freed with a base open to bring up Schmidt, who had flied out and grounded out his first two at-bats. Schmidt made them pay for the decision to walk Freed; he ripped a three-run shot for his first home run, giving the Phillies a 3–1 lead they never relinquished.

Schmidt played a total of 13 games in September, getting seven starts at third base and one at second base. He had seven hits in 34 at-bats for a .206 average, and the homer against Montreal was his only extra-base hit. He struck out 15 times, including three times in the final game of the season against young Chicago Cubs pitcher Bill Bonham. Many observers thought Schmidt could not handle big-league pitching; he seemed overmatched. But the team's player personnel department felt differently. They had seen enough from Schmidt in the minors to determine he would be a long-term solution at third base.

"Baseball guys are taught to break the tools down, and if you break Schmitty down as a young guy, he was a five-tool player," said Dallas Green, who was the director of minor leagues for the Phillies in 1972. "He could run like hell. He could steal bases. He had a great arm. He could field with the best of them, and he could hit and hit with power."

Schmidt was taking over as the starting third baseman for a team that was known as the perennial loser of the National League. The Phillies had never won a World Series, losing in their only two trips to the Fall Classic in 1915 and 1950. They were coming off consecutive last-place finishes and five straight losing seasons. In some ways, the Phillies still had not recovered from the infamous collapse of 1964.

Young manager Gene Mauch had a talented team that year. Right fielder Johnny Callison and rookie third baseman Richie Allen provided the power in the lineup. Scrappy infielders Tony Taylor, Bobby Wine, Ruben Amaro, and Cookie Rojas were steady fielders who helped the Phillies win games with their excellent defense. Future Hall of Famer Jim Bunning and Chris Short anchored a deep pitching staff.

The Phillies held a six-and-a-half-game lead over the St. Louis Cardinals with 12 games remaining. All they had to do was win four of the last 12 to capture their third pennant. But the Phillies somehow lost 10 straight games and ended up tied with the Cincinnati Reds for second place, one game behind the Cardinals.

Over the next few years, the team steadily declined. Tired of the daily operations and frustrated by the losing, owner Robert Carpenter handed over the reins of the team to his 32-year-old son, Ruly, in November 1972. Ruly Carpenter, a Yale graduate, joined the team's accounting department in 1963 and became the assistant minor league director to

Owens in 1965. When his father gave him control of the team, Ruly Carpenter was the youngest club president in the major leagues. With Owens serving as general manager and field manager and Carpenter sitting in the owner's chair, the Phillies had a new brain trust that would help lead them out of their doldrums.

"There were still serious problems with the team," Owens said. "I felt I knew what we had in the way of talent in the minors. Since I've always considered myself a good evaluator, I figured if I lived, ate, and slept with the players on the parent club, I would know just what I had, and I had confidence I could turn the thing around."

Owens was in charge of an awful team that went 59–97 and finished 37½ games out of first place in 1972. But there were several pieces in place to build around. Carlton, Bowa, Luzinski, and Montanez gave the Phillies a solid nucleus of players that already had some success in the majors. Schmidt, Boone, and pitchers Larry Christensen and Dick Ruthven were minor league prospects who provided hope for the future.

Owens returned to the front office after his brief stint as manager during the final months of the 1972 season. Bob Carpenter entrusted the Phillies to Danny Ozark in his last major move before handing the team over to his son. Ozark had played and managed in the Los Angeles Dodgers' organization for 30 years. He was considered by many to be the favorite to succeed Walter Alston as the Dodgers manager, though a hotshot minor league manager named Tommy Lasorda may have passed him over if he had stayed in Los Angeles.

Ozark was a surprise choice to manage the Phillies. Owens wanted to hire Dave Bristol, but Carpenter was convinced by vice president Bill Giles that the team needed continuity from every level in the minor leagues up to the big club. That was the formula that made the Dodgers so successful. Ozark played an important role at the Dodgers' instructional level and was viewed as the person who could nurture the young Phillies prospects.

"He was a laid-back guy," Bowa said of Ozark. "He didn't demand that much from you. He knew he had guys who policed themselves. We didn't come late. We worked hard. Some guys thought he was too aloof or laid back, but Danny basically let us play. I thought he was good for our team."

Owens made several key personnel decisions before the Phillies began their first spring training under their new manager. Looking to improve the pitching staff and clear the way for Schmidt to play third base every day, Owens traded Don Money to the Milwaukee Brewers for pitchers Jim Lonborg and Ken Brett. Schmidt was playing winter ball in Puerto Rico when one of his teammates rushed to his room with the news that Money had been traded. Schmidt knew the move meant the Phillies had enough confidence in him to give him the starting job. But the Phillies later added veteran backup Cesar Tovar to provide insurance, so Schmidt hadn't yet been given the keys to the kingdom.

Owens also acquired center fielder Del Unser from the Cleveland Indians, moved Montanez to first base, and named Boone the starting catcher. When Ozark arrived in Clearwater, Florida, for his first spring training as a major league manager, he made it clear to his young team that he would emphasize the fundamentals. That was the Dodgers way, and the Phillies needed improvement in that area. First, Ozark had to convince the players to do things his way.

Ozark was not a popular pick to be the new manager. The players would have preferred Dave Bristol or Jim Bunning, the two candidates who were rumored to be getting the job. Fans wanted a familiar face like Bunning or Richie Ashburn. Ozark never played in the major leagues and was a journeyman first baseman who languished in the minors. He was not a good public speaker and had a penchant for malaprops. But Ozark's goal was to help teach the young Phillies how to play the game the right way, and he treated Schmidt as a special project.

"I wasn't ready for the big leagues," Schmidt said. "My good year in Triple A had earned me the September call-up in 1972, but after only a year and a half in the minors, I wasn't ready. You need to understand that the Pacific Coast League, back then, probably was not as tough as the AA Eastern League where I started and flopped in 1971. But fortunately—for me, at least—the Phillies, who hadn't had a winning season since 1967, had nothing to lose, so they opened the door for me."

From the moment he heard the Phillies had traded Don Money, Schmidt was excited to start the 1973 season. He showed up at spring training eager to prove the Phillies made the right decision by clearing the way for him to play third base. Opening Day is always special for baseball players, and Schmidt was looking forward to his first.

But those plans went awry late in spring training when Schmidt injured his shoulder in an exhibition game against the Cincinnati Reds. Slugger Tony Perez ripped a ball down the line, and Schmidt dove hard to his right to make the play. He backhanded the ball and landed hard on his left shoulder. Schmidt laid on the ground in foul territory, writhing in pain until he passed out. Trainer Don Seger rushed out and used smelling salts to bring Schmidt around, but realized there was a more serious problem. Schmidt had dislocated his shoulder. Seger held Schmidt's arm tightly and shoved the shoulder back into its socket.

"You ain't seen nothing until you look down and see your arm coming out the front of your shoulder," Schmidt said.

When the Phillies broke camp and headed north to start the season, Schmidt stayed behind in Florida. He was expected to miss up to six weeks. Instead, he was ready to go in less than a month. Schmidt missed 10 games before making his season debut against the St. Louis Cardinals at Veterans Stadium on April 21. Batting sixth behind Bill Robinson, Schmidt singled in four at-bats in Philadelphia's 7–4 victory. He was 1-for-4 with two strikeouts in a 4–2 win the next night. In his third game, Schmidt got to face Bob Gibson, the same guy whose picture hung on Schmidt's bedroom wall at Ohio University.

Gibson was in the twilight of his career, but he was still a dominant pitcher. The hard-throwing right-hander had already won more than 200 games, two National League Cy Young Awards, and one Most Valuable Player Award and had helped lead the Cardinals to two World Series championships. Schmidt could not believe it when he saw his name and Gibson's name on the same lineup card.

"Bob Gibson! I had watched this guy dominate hitters for 15 years. I had owned and cherished his baseball card for 10 years," Schmidt said. "And now, in only the [third] game of my rookie year, I was standing in the batter's box, looking out at the legend himself. Was I a little uneasy? You could say so."

Gibson overpowered Schmidt with high fastballs and fooled him with nasty sliders, striking him out twice. With the score tied at 1–1, Schmidt came up again with two outs in the bottom of the ninth inning. Gibson fell behind in the count 2–1 and threw another slider low and away. Schmidt somehow reached out and hooked a line drive over the left-field fence to win the game and fulfill his prophecy.

"I circled the bases to a standing ovation, and as I rounded third Mr. Gibson was making his way toward the third-base line on his way to the dugout," Schmidt said. "I didn't know what to do, so I slowed my home run trot to let him pass in front of me."

Schmidt got off to a decent start as the Phillies played .500 ball in April. After going 1-for-3 against Houston on May 1, Schmidt's batting average reached .276, but it was all downhill from there. Schmidt struggled with his hitting throughout the rest of the season. Ozark met with Owens and Dallas Green once every homestand to discuss Schmidt's performance. Green and Owens wanted to send Schmidt back to Triple A, but Ozark pushed hard to keep him in the big leagues.

"The common sense thing would've been to send him down, but Danny fought for him," Green said. "Danny wanted to keep him and you have to give Danny a lot of credit for that. He recognized that this guy was going to be that good, and we weren't going anywhere anyway. You have to have patience with those guys. Pope [Owens] had the patience and Danny had the foresight to see this was gonna be his guy."

Ozark figured Schmidt would benefit more by learning from his mistakes in the majors than having more success against lesser talent in the minors.

"Mike had proven he could hit Triple-A pitching; what was he going to prove down there?" Ozark said. "I said to Owens, 'We might as well let him play.' He had great hands, quick reactions, and his swing was like a Ben Hogan golf swing. The ball came off the bat like a rocket. He didn't muscle the ball. It was all timing and bat speed. He had so much talent, it was only a matter of time before he put it all together."

Schmidt struck out so much his first season—136 times in 367 at-bats—that some of his teammates mocked him. Montanez, a flamboyant player known for his showboating, would walk past Schmidt and pretend to sneeze, suggesting that he caught a cold from the draft caused by all those missed swings. Bowa, who razzed many of his teammates, picked on Schmidt more than others. Schmidt eventually became depressed and questioned whether he could really play at the major league level. The front office became concerned over Schmidt's mental makeup.

"We were worried about that," Green said. "But by Danny showing confidence in him and playing him every day regardless of what happened, he came to realize that he can play and he just had to make some adjustments and make some improvements at the plate and he would be fine."

Ozark took a paternalistic approach with Schmidt, summoning him to his office almost on a daily basis for conversations and advice. He even benched Schmidt against some of the tougher right-handed pitchers. Ozark began calling Schmidt "Dutch," which is a term of endearment for players of German ancestry. But Schmidt resented the nickname because he thought it implied that he was dumb.

"He thought I was a stubborn kid," Schmidt said later in his career. "He treated me more like my father, disciplining me, yelling at me, using me as an example."

It wasn't until several years later that Schmidt realized Ozark only meant well; the manager just had a unique way of showing how much he cared. "I had my problems with Danny Ozark bothering me the whole year, sometimes I thought too much," Schmidt said. "I love Danny Ozark for caring about me as much as he did, but I'm not sure the way he cared about me helped me that year."

Off the field, Schmidt really lived it up his rookie season, partying hard almost every night. No matter how he played, he found an excuse to go out. If he did well, he went out to celebrate; if he played poorly, he went out to forget his struggles. All the partying drained him and he often slept through the day, waking up just in time to get to the ballpark.

"The Phillies weren't in contention to win any titles that year, and it seemed like we had most of our fun—did most of our damage—after the ballgames," Schmidt said. "Weren't many nights went by we weren't sleeping in the next morning until 1:00 or 2:00 for having not gone to bed until the wee hours of the morning, just living the life of a big leaguer, a big leaguer with no responsibilities."

That all changed quickly. On some occasions, Schmidt woke up early enough to play golf with Steve Carlton and some of his other teammates. It was after one of those outings that he met a waitress named Donna Wightman. She was more interested in music and her singing career than baseball, but Schmidt asked Donna to go on a date and the two hit it off right away. There would be no more late-night partying for Schmidt. Now he had someone to spend time with away from baseball. Donna was a good listener and she had strong perspective. There was more to life than baseball, and having Donna around him helped Schmidt understand that.

Toward the end of his rookie year, Schmidt was struggling to keep his batting average above .200. He was hitting .209 going into the final week, but then he went 0-for-13 in three games against the Pittsburgh Pirates. His average dropped to .201 entering a final weekend series at St. Louis. Schmidt went 0-for-2 with two walks in the first game to slip to .200. Next up was Bob Gibson. Schmidt walked and fouled out against Gibson, but he struck out twice facing reliever Orlando Pena to drop to .198. In the final game, Schmidt was 0-for-4 with three strikeouts to finish with a .196 batting average. He finished the season hitless in his last 26 at-bats.

Despite his struggles during his up-and-down season, Schmidt earned respect from teammates and opponents. "You remind me of Henry Aaron, the way you swing the bat," Chicago Cubs Hall of Fame shortstop Ernie Banks told Schmidt after a game at Wrigley Field that year.

Even Bowa, who gave Schmidt a hard time, looks back on that year and gives him credit for everything he endured. "He came across as confident, not cocky," Bowa said. "Watching him his first year in the big leagues, you knew he was going to be something special even though he hit under .200. He hit some balls that I've never seen guys hit before. I didn't know he was gonna be a Hall of Famer, but I knew he was going to be a great power hitter. I respected him after I watched him the first year. To do what he did hitting under .200, it was pretty special, especially with people being on him. He took a lot of heat."

Schmidt got along with many teammates, but his relationship with Bowa was never a close one. Bowa was signed as an amateur free agent by the Phillies in 1965 and he had scratched and clawed for everything he earned in the major leagues. Schmidt, on the other hand, was perceived as the cool, confident big shot who got everything handed to him on a silver platter. Still, the two players were able to coexist peacefully and they had some good times together over the years.

"Bull [Greg Luzinski], Boone, and those guys knew my personality, but I don't think Schmitty knew me," Bowa said. "You couldn't kid around with Schmitty the way you could with Bull, Boone, or Bake McBride. Everybody laughed. Schmitty, you would have to watch your timing of it. If he was going bad, you would have to lay off. He didn't take offense to it, though."

Schmidt said he thought Bowa harbored "some inner jealousy" toward him. "It took me probably five or six years to get into good graces with Larry Bowa as an individual," Schmidt said.

Bowa admired Schmidt, even if it did not always seem that way to the young third baseman. "It took a while for us to know each other," he said. "We did little things, too. We'd play basketball, we'd play golf, we'd bowl. He was unbelievable. He was great at it. I saw him throwing a football and he'd fire it real long. He could shoot a basketball. He could do anything in any sport and be successful at it."

After the season ended, Schmidt spent two weeks with Ozark working in the batting cages at Veterans Stadium. Schmidt was reluctant to do the extra work because the season was over, but he went along with it. Ozark and others knew that Schmidt's problem was probably more mental than physical. He was a classic overthinker, even at a young age.

"He always did that," Green said. "He always drove us crazy with that. God bless him. He got a bit stubborn, but not until he had some big-league time. He was stubborn in making adjustments and understanding hitting."

Ozark was optimistic the time he spent with Schmidt after the season would benefit him in the future. "At first, I think Mike resented my postseason instruction, but he got over it when he realized the practice was for his own benefit," Ozark said. "Nor was there anything drastic about the change I suggested in his hitting. It was just a slight change in the way he held the bat and his stance. The ability was there. It was just a matter of improving his concentration."

The roller-coaster season took a major toll on Schmidt's confidence. "I had none at the end of that year," he said. "I was back at ground zero. I didn't have any major injuries, any serious health problems to worry about, but in terms of performance, I went from being on top in Triple A, thinking I was going to turn right into a Rookie of the Year candidate the next year in the big leagues, to wondering if I was even going to make it in the big leagues inside of a year."

With his confidence shattered, Schmidt reported to Caguas, Puerto Rico, to play winter ball in the off-season for a team managed by Bobby Wine, one of Ozark's coaches who played shortstop for the 1964 Phillies. Wine took the opposite approach toward Schmidt; he was more soft-spoken than Ozark and offered positive reinforcement.

"You sting the ball when you hit, Mike," Wine told him. "But you also strike out too often. Remember, when you're up with a man in scoring position, you don't have to drive the ball 700 feet. Just hit it to right center or left center. You're a good player, a good hitter."

Wine's team was loaded with talented players, including Gary Carter, Larry Christensen, and Jim Essian. They advanced to the Latin American World Series that winter. Following Wine's advice, Schmidt was more relaxed at the plate and cut down his swing. He also became more aggressive, taking fewer pitches than he did his rookie season.

"All these years I've thought you had to swing hard to hit it far," Schmidt told Wine. "Trying to hit it far by swinging hard, that's what created all my problems. Now I know you can swing easy and get the same results."

Schmidt's new approach gave him more confidence at the plate. Now he was ready for a breakout season.

"My relationship with Bobby Wine in the formative years of my career, getting to know him and going to winter ball and playing under him, played as big a role in turning my career around as anything," Schmidt said.

CHAPTER **3**

The All-Star

"When I came to the Phillies in 1974, Mike had all the tools but he didn't have the confidence. He was constantly doubting himself. And the fans rode him pretty hard. I spent a lot of time with him, trying to get him to block out the crowd."

—Dave Cash

After his disappointing rookie season, Mike Schmidt just wanted to prove he belonged in the major leagues. An impressive performance in winter ball gave him more confidence, and he was ready to carry it over to the Phillies.

Shortly before Schmidt arrived in Clearwater for spring training in 1974, he married his girlfriend, Donna Wightman, at his parents' home in Dayton before a small gathering of family and friends. He had a new bride and a new attitude. Now it was time to put it all together.

"Last year, I was single, and I'd never go home right after a game," Schmidt said. "Sometimes I'd be out until all hours of the morning. Things are different now that I have a wife to go home to. I'm not concerned with anything now except baseball and loving my wife."

But Schmidt's mood took a drastic turn for the worse once he walked into the batting cage for the first time in Clearwater to hit against a pitching machine. Manager Danny Ozark was there waiting for him with a bit of unexpected and unwanted advice.

"I've been thinking about the way you uppercut the ball and I want you to try something different," Ozark said. "I want you to hold the bat the way Nate Colbert does. I want you to start with it level instead of holding it upright."

Colbert was a power hitter for the San Diego Padres who slugged 38 home runs in 1970 and 1972. He was coming off a season in which he batted a career-best .270 with 22 homers and 80 RBIs. But Colbert was also prone to striking out. He whiffed 146 times in 1973 and had averaged 133 strikeouts over the previous five seasons. Nonetheless, Ozark wanted Schmidt to emulate Colbert's odd stance in which he held the bat on his shoulder. Schmidt was not pleased because he thought he had made a lot of progress working with Bobby Wine in winter ball. He was surprised that Ozark wanted him to make such a dramatic change to his batting stance. This was not a minor tweak; any player would need time to get comfortable with such an adjustment.

"Look, Danny," Schmidt said. "I want to be left alone. Right now I'm a good hitter. I have a good stroke and I don't want to mess with it. I'm staying on the ball, not yanking away. I've learned to relax."

Ozark would not hear it. "Yo, Dutch," he replied. "A .196 hitter can't be stubborn. Try it my way."

Schmidt was angry. He resisted the urge to snap back at his manager and jumped in the cage. Gripping the bat tightly, he felt awkward with this new stance, and it showed when he swung and missed at the first pitch he saw. He immediately dropped the bat and stormed out of the cage, muttering, "I can't hit that way."

Ozark threatened to demote Schmidt to the minors if he did not change his hitting approach. This time, Schmidt refused to back down from a confrontation. "I'm not changing. So go ahead and send me to Triple A," he told his manager. Schmidt wanted to swing soft and put the ball in play the way he did with success in Puerto Rico.

"A hitter's stance in the batter's box is personal, like his bat," Schmidt later explained. "If I gave you a bat and asked you to stand at home plate, you'd pick a spot in relation to the plate where you'd instinctively stand if someone was going to throw you a pitch. That's the first thing a player should do: walk into the batter's box and stand where his instincts tell him to. From that point, he should adjust his stance based on the kind of hitter he is or feels he can be."

Hoping to avoid more conflict, Schmidt turned to bullpen coach Carroll Beringer, who served as a liaison between the players and the manager. Schmidt asked Beringer if he could get Ozark to back off a bit. The message made its way to Ozark and the coaching staff. Wine took Schmidt's side and suggested the young slugger should be left alone. "The more hollering and screaming we do, the more confused he's gonna get," Wine said.

Ozark agreed to grant Schmidt his wish. He cut back on his lectures and did not tinker with his batting stance anymore. He stayed quiet when Schmidt messed up at the plate or in the field, and complimented him when he did well.

Without the constant criticism from Ozark, Schmidt was able to relax and focused on improving his game. A new teammate helped his psyche tremendously. During the off-season, the Phillies made an important trade that not only improved the team on the field but reshaped the chemistry in the clubhouse. Sensing the need for veteran leadership, general manager Paul Owens traded pitcher Ken Brett to the Pittsburgh Pirates for second baseman Dave Cash. Though he was only 26, Cash already knew how to win and he had a strong clubhouse presence. Cash replaced Bill Mazeroski in Pittsburgh and played on a team that won three division titles and one World Series.

Upon joining his new team, Cash made an immediate impact, providing leadership and instilling much-needed confidence. He coined the team's rallying cry: "Yes we can!" Cash had great influence on Schmidt, constantly encouraging the youngster and helping him stay focused.

"When I came to the Phillies in 1974, Mike had all the tools but he didn't have the confidence," Cash said. "He was constantly doubting himself. And the fans rode him pretty hard. I spent a lot of time with him, trying to get him to block out the crowd."

Veteran Bill Robinson also provided strong support for Schmidt. Robinson was labeled the "next Mickey Mantle" as a young player, but had failed to live up to those enormous expectations with the New York Yankees and bounced around the league. He knew how difficult it was to play under constant pressure and counseled Schmidt about dealing with it.

Schmidt would not let his teammates down. Right from the start, he hit the cover off the ball in 1974. On Opening Day at Veterans Stadium, the Phillies trailed the New York Mets 4–3 in the bottom of the ninth inning when Schmidt came to the plate against closer Tug McGraw. There was one out and the tying run was on second base. Schmidt, who was batting in the eighth spot that is usually reserved for light hitters, was looking to hit a single and send the game into extra innings. Instead, he ripped a two-run home run to left field to win the game. That hit set the tone for an outstanding season.

Schmidt batted .338 in April and reached .340 by mid-May. Ozark kept Schmidt in the eight-hole in the lineup for most of the first month before finally moving him up to sixth and eventually third, where he stayed for most of the year. Schmidt's power had been evident from the moment he came up to the big leagues, but he really started showing it on a consistent basis in his second year. In a game against the San Francisco Giants at the Vet on June 1, Schmidt hit a mighty blast off lefty Mike Caldwell that landed in the third row of the upper deck in section 575, an amazing seven sections over from the left-field foul pole. The ball traveled an estimated 441 feet.

Fans around the country became aware of Schmidt's impressive power later that month when he slammed a long drive off a speaker high along the roof of the Houston Astrodome in a game against the Astros on June 10. Engineers at the dome estimated the ball might have traveled 500 to 600 feet had the speaker not blocked it. Schmidt settled for a single on his towering shot off pitcher Claude Osteen, but the national attention he received made up for losing a homer.

"I never saw a ball hit so hard in my life," Astros center fielder Cesar Cedeno said after the game.

By mid-June, Schmidt was hitting .315 with 16 home runs and 47 RBIs. He was a legitimate candidate to make the National League All-Star team, less than half a season after he batted .196. The only problem was that Schmidt had been left off the All-Star ballot because of his poor rookie season. The Phillies initiated a write-in campaign and Howard Eskin, a young engineer at a local radio station, wrote Schmidt's name on 30,000 ballots himself. The team hired a helicopter to airlift 100,000 ballots to All-Star headquarters, and Schmidt ended up with the most write-in votes in the history of All-Star voting. Still, he finished second behind Ron Cey of the Los Angeles Dodgers in the voting. But National League manager Yogi Berra chose Schmidt as a backup for the squad.

"The guy is having a fantastic year," Berra said. "Besides, I don't want to get shot next time I go to Philly."

Cash, Steve Carlton, and Larry Bowa joined Schmidt at the All-Star Game, which was played in Pittsburgh's Three Rivers Stadium. Schmidt came to the plate twice and walked both times. He scored one run in the National League's 7–2 victory.

With Schmidt and Cash leading the way, the Phillies made a strong bid to go from worst to first in the division. They spent a total of 70 days in first place and were atop the standings as late as August 2. But the

Pirates eventually caught the Phillies, and Philadelphia finished eight games behind Pittsburgh in third place with an 80–82 record. It was the first time the team had finished higher than fifth since 1966. This was a sign of better years to come.

Schmidt batted .282, an 86-point improvement from a year earlier. He led the National League with 36 home runs and a .546 slugging percentage, drove in 116 runs, and stole 23 bases. Schmidt also led the league with 138 strikeouts. He played all 162 games, and his defense improved so much that he finished second in the voting for the Gold Glove Award.

"I guess I just learned to relax," Schmidt explained. "Last year I was in and out of the lineup, and when I was in I probably tried too hard to do well because I was wondering if I'd be in the next day. I wanted to relax last season, but I couldn't. I was as tight as a drum. This year, when I go to the plate, I'd say 70 to 80 percent of the time, I'm at ease just looking to hit the ball hard somewhere. When you come up to the plate that way, your natural instincts take over."

Cash batted .300 that season and Larry Bowa raised his average from .211 to .275, giving the Phillies a formidable middle-infield combination. Willie Montanez rebounded from two disappointing seasons to hit .304, though his power continued to decrease as he had only seven homers. Bob Boone showed he could be a regular starting catcher in the majors. Greg Luzinski missed most of the year with a knee injury, but the slugger drove in 48 runs in 85 games.

The Phillies had solid hitters to surround Schmidt in the lineup and he had strong support in the clubhouse from Cash and Robinson.

"Before those guys came to the Phillies, it wasn't too much fun to come to the ballpark," he said. "Robbie had a lot to do with the early success in my career. He was one of the first guys who gave me a lot of confidence by telling me that I was a good player and that I was going to be successful someday. Dave Cash also helped me in terms of having a good, positive attitude around the clubhouse. He always seemed to say the right things to me. That was a big difference from guys like Bowa, Luzinski, and Montanez, who were ragging on me all the time, kidding me about striking out. There was a bit of jealousy there and I saw it as mean-spirited, no question."

Some of the resentment toward Schmidt was understandable. Montanez was "the man" on the Phillies before Schmidt arrived. He finished second in the NL Rookie of the Year voting in 1971 when he had 30 homers and 99 RBIs. He had a flamboyant style on the field and was popular with fans, who called him "Willie the Phillie." But Montanez struggled to produce after his outstanding rookie season, and Schmidt's presence added to the pressure he felt.

Luzinski was a year younger than Schmidt and he also had an excellent rookie year in 1972, hitting .281 with 18 homers and 68 RBIs. But Luzinski, nicknamed "the Bull," was a big guy who battled weight problems. He was listed at 225 pounds—though that seemed understated—and Luzinski could not match Schmidt's athletic skills.

Bowa and Schmidt were complete opposites. While Schmidt was cool and had a laid-back attitude, Bowa was a fiery, aggressive agitator. He had to fight to make it to the majors and felt he needed to keep proving himself each and every year.

"Larry was a great clubhouse needler, but he didn't have great timing," Schmidt said. "There were times when he didn't needle people and I think he should have. There were times when he needled me that I thought it would be best to lay off. One time, I got so angry in a clubhouse in Houston that I almost wanted to kill him. I probably would have if there weren't four other players there to separate us."

* * *

Schmidt found an unexpected mentor in 1975. One month into the season, the Phillies acquired Dick Allen from the Atlanta Braves, bringing back the controversial slugger who was the National League Rookie of the Year in 1964 when he played in Philadelphia. Schmidt played a major role in orchestrating the reunion.

Allen was the first African American star to play for the Phillies and his first stint with the team was marked by heavy racial tension. The Phillies were the last National League team to integrate after Jackie

Robinson broke the color barrier with the Brooklyn Dodgers in 1947. They did not have a black player until John Kennedy played in five games at third base in 1957. The team did not regularly field black players until the mid-1960s when Bill White, Johnny Briggs, and Allen arrived in town.

Allen gained respect from all of his teammates—black and white— for his exceptional skills, but he had a rough time in Philadelphia for several reasons. Allen was an opinionated man and he spoke out against racism in a city that was racially segregated. He also managed to find himself in the center of controversy for a variety of issues. In 1965, Allen was involved in a fight with teammate Frank Thomas, a popular white player. The Phillies released Thomas the following day, and fans blamed Allen. They booed him every night, threw trash at him in the outfield, and sent him hate mail. It was so dangerous that Allen wore a batting helmet in the field. The press treated Allen harshly and annoyed him by calling him Richie, and not Dick as he preferred.

After the 1969 season, Allen demanded a trade and was sent to the St. Louis Cardinals. He lasted just one season with the Cardinals and played one year with the Los Angeles Dodgers before going to the Chicago White Sox. Allen played three seasons with the White Sox, winning the American League Most Valuable Player Award in 1972 and leading the league in home runs twice. Allen left the White Sox with two weeks remaining in the 1974 season, citing a feud with teammate Ron Santo as the reason. He was traded to the Braves in December but decided to retire instead.

Only 32 at the time he quit, Allen returned to his farm in Perkasie, Pennsylvania, to raise thoroughbred horses. But the Phillies thought he could still play and they needed a power hitter to bat fifth behind Schmidt and Luzinski. Allen hit .301 with 32 homers and 88 RBIs in his last year with the White Sox; many felt if he had another season like that in Philadelphia, the Phillies could win the division.

During an off day in April, Schmidt, Cash, and broadcaster Richie Ashburn went to visit Allen on his farm. "I'll never forget playing horse—with a basketball, not a thoroughbred—on an old hoop hanging in his barn while we talked about how well he'd fit in on the Phillies," Schmidt said.

The visit left a strong impression on Allen, who really felt wanted by a team for the first time in his career. "It was a conversation I wouldn't forget," Allen said. "Schmidt was talking about the Phils needing some additional clout, a big stick in the lineup to go with his and Luzinski's. He said something about 'Schmidt-Luzinski-Allen firepower.' Cash was rapping about the brothers on the Phils' team and how they could use a veteran to inspire them. And ol' Richie Ashburn was telling tales about how much the city of Philadelphia had changed for the better. That was as specific as it got, but I got the message: 'Come home, Dick. We love you. They're gonna love you!'

"At first I figured it had to be a joke. It's not my style to return to the scene of the crime. But I had to admit the idea of coming home did fire me up a bit. I always did like surprises—even when the surprises were on me. When they left the farm that day, I hugged them all. I was touched to feel wanted by guys who played for the Phillies."

Allen said he would think about returning to play, and soon after that visit Ashburn came back to the farm with Hall of Fame pitcher Robin Roberts. Convinced it was the right time for a reconciliation and excited about the possibility of playing for a team that had a chance to win a World Series, Allen decided to end his retirement. Schmidt was thrilled one of his heroes was going to be his teammate.

"Growing up, I admired Dick Allen," he said. "I pretended I was like him when I was up at bat playing Legion ball in Ohio. I was fortunate that we became good friends on the Phillies and that I learned a lot from him."

To clear room for Allen to play first base, Paul Owens traded Montanez to the San Francisco Giants for center fielder Garry Maddox. The move benefited the Phillies because Maddox was an outstanding defensive player and a solid hitter. He also became Schmidt's best friend on the team.

"We shared in something far larger than baseball," Schmidt said. "We grew close as we searched for our spiritual lives together, and we did charity work in the community. He was—still is—the most unselfish person I've ever met."

By the time Maddox and Allen arrived, the Phillies were hovering around the .500 mark, not the kind of start they envisioned. Schmidt was downright awful. He batted .164 with two homers in April and looked completely lost at the plate. After a breakout season, Schmidt had reverted to his rookie form. He was striking out at an astounding pace. Critics said Schmidt thought too much, and manager Danny Ozark agreed.

"Schmitty, if you were dumb you'd be better off," he told his third baseman. "There have been a lot of great dumb ballplayers, some of them so dumb they couldn't even remember yesterday."

Fans gave Schmidt a hard time and the writers could not understand how he could be so unemotional after all those strikeouts. They nicknamed him "Captain Cool." While players like Bowa would slam helmets and throw bats when things went wrong, Schmidt simply walked back to the dugout and put his bat in the rack.

"Mike didn't show his emotions," Bowa said. "Even Bull would throw his bat sometimes like I would. Maybe the way he answered questions sometimes, he seemed aloof. But I was in the locker room with him. He wanted to win as bad as I did. He just didn't show it that way. He had a way of just trying to keep everything under control no matter if he was 0-for-32, and I think that hurt. I think he sometimes wondered why I got away with shit, but I let it all out. I'd show it. If I was happy, I'd show it. If I was mad, I'd show it. Schmitty, early in his career, you didn't know if he was happy or sad. He was just the same."

Billy DeMars, the Phillies' batting coach, worked tirelessly with Schmidt in the batting cages. He understood that Schmidt came across as a nonchalant player, but DeMars realized that the youngster was actually trying *too* hard. "He hits the ball great in batting practice because he's nice and easy and relaxed," DeMars said. "But in the game he tightens up, trying to hit the ball hard."

Schmidt was still batting under .200 as late as June 9 and Ozark soon dropped him from third to sixth in the batting order. But with Demars' help, Schmidt started turning things around in early July. He raised his average from .212 to .243 in a span of 11 games in which he had at least two hits eight times. Schmidt batted .278 after the All-Star break and finished the season with a .249 average and 95 RBIs. His home runs increased to 38, which again led the league. But his strikeouts also went up to 180.

"Billy DeMars really worked his ass off and helped him develop," Dallas Green said. "He worked hours and hours with him. He was a little stubborn, Mr. Cool. It was that makeup thing that we were all worried about it throughout his career, but he always did something to rise to the occasion to make us back off."

The Phillies stayed in contention most of the season, but did not really threaten the Pirates for the division title. They finished in second place with 86 wins, 6½ games behind Pittsburgh.

Cash and Bowa each hit .305 and Luzinski had a monster season, batting .300 with 34 homers and 120 RBIs. Maddox batted .291, right fielder Jay Johnstone hit .329, and Allen chipped in with 12 homers and 62 RBIs in 119 games. Ozark was frustrated his talented squad had a disappointing year. Shortly before the season ended, he blasted Schmidt.

"He's not doing himself any good, he's not doing the club any good, and if he doesn't get it going soon he's going to be out of a job," Ozark said. "He started off bad and instead of getting mad, gritting his teeth, and working harder, he began fighting himself. And thinking. He's thinking all the time. Now he's so confused he doesn't know what to do. And to top it off, I think he's scared of the ball. In this business, if you're scared of the ball, you've had it. I'm really afraid for him. And the management here feels the same way."

Allen helped Schmidt deal with the criticism from his manager, the press, and the fans. He was the perfect person to counsel Schmidt, having gone through many of the same things himself.

"Schmidt had as much talent as anybody I've ever seen play the game," Allen said. "Quick wrists. Strong. Perfect baseball body. But he was trying to hit every pitch out of the park, and when he didn't, he'd sulk about it.... He was moody and if he had a bad game, he'd take it home with him. I used to take him out after a game for a couple of beers and we'd talk about things, have a few laughs, put the ballyard behind us. I used to tell Schmitty to pretend he was back in the sandlots of Ohio where he grew up. Get out there and bang that ball like you did in high school. He began to get the message. He hit 38 homers in 1975 but struggled with his average. He still had some work to do."

CHAPTER 4

The Glory Years

"*I stood in front of the mirror one day and asked myself what had I done to deserve all of this success and wealth and good fortune. It just dawned on me that someone upstairs was taking good care of me. I couldn't have done it myself. At that moment a spiritual awareness came into my life.*"

—Mike Schmidt

Expectations were very high for the Phillies entering the bicentennial season of 1976. They proved they could compete in the division in 1974 and 1975. Now it was time to take the next step and win the National League East.

General manager Paul Owens made a couple of trades at the winter meetings in December to bolster the pitching staff. The Phillies already had a potent lineup led by Mike Schmidt, but they needed another quality starting pitcher and a late-inning reliever. First, Owens acquired Ron Reed from the St. Louis Cardinals for outfielder Mike Anderson. The next day, Owens sent a package of prospects—Alan Bannister, Dick Ruthven, and Roy Thomas—to the Chicago White Sox for veteran Jim Kaat and a minor league infielder named Mike Buskey.

Reed, a 6'6" right-hander, had been a successful starter in his first eight seasons in the majors. But the Phillies moved him to the bullpen where he would eventually thrive. Kaat, a left-hander, was coming off consecutive 20-win seasons for the White Sox. Though he was 37 years old, the Phillies were counting on him to solidify the top of the rotation. Kaat even got the start on Opening Day ahead of Steve Carlton, who had not come close to matching his 27-win season in 1972.

With strong pitching to match their powerful offense, the Phillies figured to be one of the top teams in the National League. But they stumbled out of the gate, losing three of their first four games. Schmidt was not helping. He had three hits in 18 at-bats and struck out nine times. Once again, manager Danny Ozark dropped Schmidt from third to sixth in the batting order before the Phillies played the Chicago Cubs at Wrigley Field on April 17. Schmidt was not happy with the demotion; needing a pat on the back, Dick Allen provided one. He pulled Schmidt aside in the visitors' clubhouse before the game and offered some friendly advice.

"Mike, you've got to relax," Allen said. "You've got to have some fun. Remember when you were a kid and you'd skip supper to play ball? You were having fun. Hey, with all that talent you've got, baseball ought to be fun. Enjoy it. Be a kid again."

Inspired by Allen's words, Schmidt decided to go out and let his natural ability take over. He wanted to try a new bat, so he borrowed one from utility infielder Tony Taylor that was one inch shorter and one ounce lighter than his regular bat. Seldom-used infielder Terry Harmon, a fellow Ohio University alum, loaned Schmidt his ripped-up blue T-shirt to wear under his uniform for good luck. With a new bat, a lucky T-shirt, and a carefree attitude, Schmidt was almost a new man.

"Dick and I went on the field and tried to have some fun," Schmidt said. "Between innings, he'd throw me lob passes with the ball like a quarterback. In the dugout, we'd horse around, joke, laugh. It took my mind away from the results, and I quickly loosened up."

When Schmidt woke up that morning, he looked out of the window of his hotel to find a flag and determine which way the wind was blowing. He did that every time the Phillies played the Cubs in Chicago. Much to his delight, the wind was blowing out.

With its "friendly confines," Wrigley Field has been a hitter's ballpark since it opened in 1914. On days when the wind coming off Lake Michigan is blowing out, Wrigley can be a total nightmare for pitchers. When the wind is blowing in, it knocks down potential home runs and turns them into outs.

Carlton was on the mound for the Phillies, who needed a strong outing from their ace to get back on the winning track. But Lefty got knocked out in the second inning after allowing seven runs. After three innings, the Phillies trailed 12–1 and seemed on their way toward another loss.

Schmidt had flied out in his first at-bat against Cubs starter Rick Reuschel, but he singled leading off the fourth inning. In the fifth, Schmidt hit a two-run homer off Reuschel, but the Cubs still led 13–4. Schmidt hit a solo shot against Reuschel in the seventh, but the Phillies still trailed 13–7.

After Allen delivered a two-run single in the eighth, Schmidt blasted a three-run homer deep into the center-field bleachers off reliever Mike Garman to cut the deficit to 13–12. The Phillies scored three runs in the ninth to take a 15–13 lead, but closer Tug McGraw blew the save and the game moved to extra innings. That gave Schmidt a chance to make it four straight homers. He came up with a runner on base in the tenth inning against Paul Reuschel, Rick's older brother.

Schmidt turned on a fastball that was up and in and ripped a line drive out to left-center to give the Phillies a 17–15 lead. They held on for an 18–16 victory and Schmidt had earned himself a place in the record books. He became the 10th major leaguer to hit four home runs in one game and the first National League player to hit four in a row in modern times.

"I wasn't thinking anything special when I went up there," Schmidt said after driving in eight runs with his four homers. "I was feeling good and nice and relaxed. I don't think moving down to sixth meant anything."

"Maybe the lack of pressure helped," he said of playing from 11 runs behind. "You just go up there and work on your swing. I needed a game like this to take some of the pressure off."

The team needed to get a win almost as badly as Schmidt needed the confidence boost. The victory sparked an incredible run by the Phillies, who won 50 of their next 68 games to build a nine-game lead in the division standings by July 4, the day the country celebrated its 200th birthday. The margin was 10 games at the All-Star break as the Midsummer Classic was played at Veterans Stadium for the first time. Schmidt was joined by Bob Boone, Dave Cash, Larry Bowa, and Greg Luzinski as the Phillies' representatives. The hometown fans gave the local favorites a rousing standing ovation when they were introduced. Cash was the only Phillie to get a hit in the game, which was won by the National League 7–1.

The few days off did not slow down the Phillies. They kept winning after the short break and built their lead to 15½ games over the Pittsburgh Pirates by August 24. But the Phillies could not continue their torrid pace. Their lead slipped to 6½ games following an eight-game losing streak that began against the Cincinnati Reds on August 27. It was down to three games following a 4–3 loss in 12 innings at Wrigley Field on September 17. At that point, the entire city was in a major panic. Fans were having flashbacks to 1964, and they took out their frustrations on the players.

"A nightmare," Schmidt called it. "The hate mail, the letters saying we were choking, the abuse. I'd be out there trying to catch a tough grounder, thinking that what I did would decide whether we'd be 2½ in front the next day or 4½. *Blow this one*, I'd think, *and I'll need cops to guard my house.*"

The passionate Philadelphia fans were particularly tough on the players' families. Donna Schmidt had a terrible experience in the stands that year. "It wasn't just the booing," she said. "It's the cruel things they say. I remember when I was pregnant for the first time. Crying all the time. I was at the ballpark and this fan kept saying how ugly I was. The tears welled up in my eyes. I stayed away from the park for a long time after that."

Schmidt could not understand the mentality of Phillies fans. They booed him when he struck out and cheered when he homered. "You're trying your damnedest," he said. "You strike out and they boo you. I act like it doesn't bother me, like I don't hear anything the fans say, but the truth is I hear every word and it kills me. Our fans overreact both ways. When you're in a slump they're brutal, and when you're going good they make you come out of the dugout and tip your cap for every little thing. They're so passionate, it scares the hell out of me."

During the losing skid in September, another problem arose for the Phillies. It became apparent to many observers that the team was starting to become racially divided. There was one clique of white players and another that consisted of black players: Allen, Cash, Garry Maddox, Ollie Brown, and Bobby Tolan. Bowa exacerbated the problem by constantly criticizing Allen for the first baseman's inability to dig out balls in the dirt; Allen countered by telling the shortstop to make better throws. Schmidt was caught in the middle because he was closer with the black players. He had never judged anyone based on skin color and always viewed people equally.

"Growing up, the athletes I admired were Jim Brown, Frank Robinson, Oscar Robertson, Walt Frazier," Schmidt said, naming some of the best black players in various sports. "And then it happened that my best friends on the Phillies were black. I feel guys become friends because they have similar interests. And I've learned a lot from Garry and Dick."

In the end, the racial issues did not hinder the Phillies. They eventually turned things around in September and finished with a franchise-record 101 wins to clinch their first postseason berth in 26 years. A 4–1 victory over the Montreal Expos in the first game of a doubleheader sealed the National League East crown for the Phillies with seven games remaining on the schedule.

After the game, while the rest of the team poured champagne and celebrated, Schmidt, Allen, Maddox, and Cash gathered quietly in an equipment room. Allen offered a prayer of thanks that the four players had shared the season together before they joined the party with the rest of their teammates. Some players were peeved the four players were absent, and McGraw addressed the situation in a team meeting later. "Tug brought it up, but it's dead now," Schmidt said. "It wasn't a good scene, but it's over."

The Phillies had more pressing concerns, namely trying to find a way to beat the defending World Series champion Cincinnati Reds in the National League Championship Series. The Big Red Machine boasted a formidable lineup that featured All-Stars Pete Rose, Joe Morgan, Johnny Bench, George Foster, Dave Concepcion, Tony Perez, and Ken Griffey.

But the Phillies had the pitching that could offset Cincinnati's offense, especially in a best-of-five series. Carlton won 20 games and had a 3.13 ERA. Jim Lonborg had 18 wins and a 3.08 ERA. Kaat (12–14, 3.48), Larry Christensen (13–8, 3.67), and Tom Underwood (10–5, 3.52) rounded out an outstanding rotation.

Philadelphia also had the hitters to compete with Cincinnati's offensive firepower. Schmidt, Luzinski, and Maddox had terrific seasons. Schmidt batted .262 with 38 homers and 107 RBIs. Maddox hit .330 and stole 29 bases. Luzinski slammed 21 homers, drove in 95 runs, and hit .304. Jay Johnstone batted .318.

The series opened at Veterans Stadium with Carlton facing left-hander Don Gullett. The city was buzzing in anticipation of the Phillies' first playoff game since the Whiz Kids lost to the New York Yankees in the 1950 World Series. Schmidt's sacrifice fly in the bottom of the first gave the Phillies a 1–0 lead, but the Reds went ahead in the sixth on a Foster home run and won the game 6–3.

Lonborg could not hold a 2–0 lead in Game 2, allowing the Reds to rally for four runs in the sixth inning. Reliever Pedro Borbon shut down the Phillies, tossing four scoreless innings after starter Pat Zachry departed, and the Reds won 6–2 to put the Phillies on the verge of elimination.

Hoping to avoid a sweep, the Phillies traveled to Cincinnati for Game 3 at Riverfront Stadium. They had a 3–0 lead going into the bottom of the seventh inning, but Kaat and Ron Reed combined to give up four runs. The Phillies answered with two runs in the eighth and one in the ninth to go up 6–4. But Foster and Bench hit back-to-back homers off Reed to tie it in the bottom of the ninth. Gene Garber came in and allowed a single to Concepcion, and the Reds shortstop scored the winning run on Griffey's single off Underwood to end the series.

The Reds advanced to the World Series and swept the Yankees to capture their second straight championship. The Phillies went home after a breakout season looking for a way to narrow the gap between themselves and the Reds.

Schmidt won his third straight home-run title and also earned his first Gold Glove Award that season. He had a solid series against the Reds, going 4-for-13 with two doubles and two RBIs in the three games. The Phillies rewarded Schmidt with a six-year contract worth $565,000 annually, making him the highest-paid player in baseball for a brief period. Unfortunately, Schmidt also had to say good-bye to two of his best friends and confidants on the team. Shortly after the season ended, the Phillies decided to part ways with Allen. Then the team refused to give Cash a long-term contract and allowed him to sign with the Montreal Expos as a free agent.

There was a perception that Schmidt's friendship with Allen and Cash, as well as the permed hairstyle he wore in the mid-1970s, was his personal statement against the organization's treatment of black players. Schmidt strongly denied that charge.

"Sure, I may have confided in Dave Cash and Dick Allen," he said. "I respected their playing abilities, just as I did those of my other teammates. But that doesn't mean I was making a statement about race relations on the Phillies. Sure, I heard Dick talk about his experience in the minor leagues and having to stay in a separate hotel. Like anybody else—white or black—I felt badly for him that he had to deal with that kind of discrimination. But I never donned a curled hairstyle—or what some called a 'red Afro'—to show my sympathy for blacks on the team. In fact, many white players wore that kind of hairstyle in the 1970s. Bud Harrelson of the Mets was the first to try it out, and I was the second."

* * *

On the surface, it seemed that Schmidt had it all. He was a major league All-Star, he was married to a beautiful woman, he lived in a gorgeous home, and he made a ton of money playing a game he loved. But he still could not shake the feeling that something important was missing from his life.

"I stood in front of the mirror one day and asked myself what had I done to deserve all of this success and wealth and good fortune," Schmidt said. "It just dawned on me that someone upstairs was taking good care of me. I couldn't have done it myself. At that moment a spiritual awareness came into my life. It didn't come out of a tragedy or a need. No fireworks went off. But I decided I ought to put the credit somewhere. I became a believer in a supreme being. I had been always out for myself, for No. 1, willing to advance at the expense of others, do anything to get to the top, to the major leagues, to wealth."

Schmidt began attending Bible study classes during the winter of 1976 with teammate Jim Kaat and Philadelphia 76ers general manager Pat Williams. He continued his spiritual pursuit during the season by going to Baseball Chapel on Sundays. Baseball Chapel was founded by

Detroit sportswriter Watson Spoelstra in 1972. It is a nondenominational Christian ministry that is committed to the spiritual development of people throughout professional baseball. Baseball Chapel organizes Sunday services for both home and away teams in clubhouses across the majors, and is open to players, coaches, managers, wives, umpires, front office staff, and ballpark employees.

Schmidt was first encouraged to attend Baseball Chapel by teammate Bob Boone. The Phillies were among several teams with a strong Christian influence, and about 15 to 20 players regularly attend the weekly chapel service. Schmidt and Boone had formed a relationship when they first started playing together in the minors, and they grew closer through religion. Schmidt also found fellowship with other Christians on the team, including Kaat and Garry Maddox.

"One Sunday I was coaxed into going to the chapel service," Schmidt said. "You have to remember that this was at a time when Baseball Chapel was considered taboo by many players. But the idea that a spiritual entity could take the pressure off of my life—that God actually wanted to take the pressure off of my life—was extremely appealing to me. So my original desire for a spiritual relationship with the Lord was more selfish than anything else. After attending Baseball Chapel on that first occasion, I found myself reading scripture more and more and reflecting on my faith. It was the beginning of my spiritual journey."

The Phillies hoped 1977 would be a journey of their own, culminating with the first World Series title in franchise history. Coming off an impressive season, the Phillies were the favorites to win the National League East again, but Philadelphia had to fill a few holes in the infield first. The Phillies signed Richie Hebner to replace Dick Allen at first base and acquired veteran Ted Sizemore from the Dodgers to take Dave Cash's spot at second base. Hebner had spent the first eight seasons of his career playing for the Pirates and had plenty of playoff experience; Sizemore was a solid player for the Cardinals and Dodgers.

Schmidt and the Phillies started slow. He batted .190 with three home runs and 18 strikeouts in 58 at-bats as the Phillies went 7–9 in April. Danny Ozark's patience with Schmidt wore thin. After Schmidt struck out three straight times in a game against Pittsburgh on April 26, the manager pinch-hit for the slugger, an unusual and humiliating move. The Phillies trailed 2–0 in the top of the eighth inning and had two runners on with one out when Ozark sent the left-handed Jay Johnstone up to face hard-throwing righty Rich Gossage. Johnstone flied out as Schmidt looked on from the dugout.

After the game, the press was more interested in discussing Ozark's strategy than the 5–0 loss. Ozark reasoned that Johnstone had a better chance of getting a hit in that situation and he did not seem concerned that Schmidt's confidence would be ruined. "It might ease things for him," Ozark said. "He might come back tomorrow with a different attitude. This could make him a bigger man than he is."

It was another awkward attempt by Ozark to motivate Schmidt, who put more pressure on himself than anyone else. Schmidt was used to the criticism and refused to engage in a verbal war with his manager. "Hey, we've only played 13 games," he said. "I haven't batted 50 times yet. Besides, my teammates have confidence in me. I know that much. They've seen me strike out three times in a row and then hit a home run. That could have happened tonight, if I had that fourth at-bat. But I can't second-guess the manager. Maybe if I was in his position, I would have done the same thing."

By mid-May, Schmidt still had not found his stroke. The Phillies were playing a little better, but they were mired in fourth place in the division. Fans let Schmidt hear it whenever he failed in a clutch situation or struck out, but he relied on his newfound spiritual strength to deal with the adversity. "I think my faith has made me more tolerant, especially of all those people who sit there and boo me," he said. "And I ask God to bless me and the players with an injury-free game."

Schmidt finally got hot in June, smacking eight home runs during an 11-game hitting streak. He continued hitting well throughout the month and raised his average to .292 following a 10-game hitting streak in early July. Schmidt's torrid hitting made him a target for pitchers. He was hit twice in three games against the New York Mets and was constantly getting brushed off the plate. After games, Schmidt would complain about it to Larry Bowa and Greg Luzinski. They did not have sympathetic ears.

"He kept coming in to the clubhouse and it was my locker, Schmitty's locker, and Bull's locker in a row, and he'd keep complaining," Larry Bowa said. "Finally, Bull said, 'Schmitty, I'm fucking tired of this shit. If you don't like it, go out there. We're gonna be behind you. The whole fucking team is gonna be behind you. Look how big you are. Go out there. It's gonna take 15 seconds and it'll stop happening.'"

The Phillies had pulled within three games of the first-place Chicago Cubs going into a game at Pittsburgh on July 8. Bruce Kison was on the mound for the Pirates. Kison was known for hitting batters and had earned the nickname "the Assassin." Schmidt came up in the seventh inning, two batters after Maddox hit a two-run homer to give the Phillies a 4–3 lead. Kison drilled him in the ribs with a fastball. Schmidt took a step toward the pitcher and said, "Next time, I'm coming after you."

Kison replied, "Why not now, big boy?" So Schmidt charged the mound and a bench-clearing brawl ensued. Pirates catcher Ed Ott tackled Schmidt from behind and Schmidt fractured the ring finger on his right hand during the altercation. Despite the injury, Schmidt had gained respect from teammates, fans, and opponents.

"It was a silly thing to do, but there comes a time when you have to assert yourself," Schmidt said. "It gets to be a question of manhood. The fans must have been wondering how much I was going to take, and I'm sure my own teammates were wondering."

Kison himself praised Schmidt afterward. "I give Schmidt credit for coming out," he said. "Talk is cheap. He backed it up. He earned my respect. I kind of enjoyed the whole thing."

The fight sparked the Pirates, who rallied to win the game by scoring four runs in the eighth and one in the ninth. Pittsburgh went on to sweep the four-game series as Schmidt was forced to sit out because of the broken finger. He returned to the lineup for the start of the next series against the St. Louis Cardinals and hit a two-run homer in a 5–4 victory. But the finger injury hampered him throughout the rest of the season.

After going back and forth with the Pirates, the Phillies moved into first place for good on August 7 with a victory over the Los Angeles Dodgers during a 13-game winning streak. They stayed there the rest of the way and won their second straight division title with another 101 victories.

Schmidt batted .274 with 38 homers and 101 RBIs, missing out on his fourth straight home-run crown to George Foster, who clubbed 52 for the Reds. Schmidt cut his strikeouts down to 122, the fewest since he entered the majors. Luzinski had an even better season, hitting .309 with 39 homers and 130 RBIs. On the pitching side, Steve Carlton won 23 games to capture his second Cy Young Award and Larry Christensen had 19 wins. With excellent hitting to support their outstanding pitching, the Phillies were ready to face the Dodgers for the National League pennant.

The Dodgers won 98 games during the season and boasted a lineup that featured All-Stars Steve Garvey, Ron Cey, and Reggie Smith. Don Sutton was the staff ace, and Doug Rau, Tommy John, and Burt Hooton gave Los Angeles a formidable rotation. Carlton faced John in Game 1 at Dodger Stadium. Luzinski's two-run homer in the first gave the Phillies a 2–0 lead, and they were up 5–1 until Cey hit a grand slam off Carlton to tie it in the bottom of the seventh.

Schmidt broke the tie with an RBI single in the ninth off reliever Elias Sosa and the Phillies added another run to earn their first postseason victory in 27 years.

In Game 2, Sutton silenced Philadelphia's bats and the Dodgers jumped on Jim Lonborg for four runs in the fourth on their way to a 7–1 win.

The series shifted to Veterans Stadium for Game 3, and the hometown crowd made its presence felt immediately. Fans pounded their feet and screamed so loudly that Hooton famously unraveled in the second inning. He walked four straight batters—including three with the bases loaded—and was booed off the mound by the raucous fans. The Phillies held a 5–3 lead going into the ninth inning and reliever Gene Garber got the first two outs easily. Pinch-hitter Vic Davalillo batted for Steve Yeager and reached on a bunt single to keep the game going. Dodgers manager Tommy Lasorda then sent up Manny Mota, his best pinch-hitter.

Throughout the season, Danny Ozark had subbed Jerry Martin for Luzinski in left field for defensive purposes late in games. But Ozark kept the slow-footed Luzinski in this time and it cost him. Mota ripped a liner to left. Luzinski broke in before scurrying back. The ball hit his glove, but it popped out as he banged into the wall. Davalillo scored on the double and Mota ended up on third base when Luzinski's throw bounced away from second baseman Ted Sizemore.

Davey Lopes followed Mota and hit a sharp grounder at Schmidt. The ball took a wicked hop off the Astroturf and bounced away toward shortstop Larry Bowa, who alertly picked it up and fired a strong throw to first base. The ball seemed to beat Lopes to the bag, but umpire Bruce Froemming called him safe. The tying run scored, and the Phillies and their fans were in disbelief.

"I'll never forget that," Bowa said. "Froemming anticipated that just because Schmitty didn't catch the ball, I couldn't throw Lopes out. I went crazy. That was the game. We win that game, we win that series."

Lopes advanced to second on an errant pickoff throw by Garber and scored on Bill Russell's single. The Dodgers won the game 6–5 and eliminated the disheartened Phillies when John outdueled Carlton in Game 4. Everyone who followed the Phillies claimed the series was lost when Froemming blew the call in Game 3, which is known as Black Friday in Philadelphia. Fans, players, and the media still do not understand why Ozark kept Luzinski in left field instead of replacing him with Martin.

"I never understood that," Bowa said. "If [Martin] is out there, we win that game. Danny had some excuse about getting Bull another at-bat in the ninth inning. But we weren't even going to bat in the ninth inning if we won."

When the Phillies and Dodgers met 31 years later in the 2008 National League Championship Series, Lopes and Bowa were on opposite sides once again. This time, Bowa wore Dodger blue as a third-base coach for manager Joe Torre and Lopes donned red pinstripes as the first-base coach for Phillies skipper Charlie Manuel. Not surprisingly, the two men still saw things differently.

"I know Davey says let it go, but he was out," Bowa said. "He knows he was out and he can go look at that all day, 100,000 times, he was out."

Lopes argued that the Phillies still had a chance to win the series after his hit tied the game in the ninth. "It wasn't the last game," he said. "They had plenty of opportunities to turn and reverse that. They didn't do it."

The series was especially hard on Schmidt because he had just one hit in 16 at-bats. He turned to his faith to help him deal with the failure. Schmidt, Maddox, Boone, Terry Harmon, and their wives and a couple players from the NBA's Philadelphia 76ers became involved in a Bible study group that was led by Wendell Kempton. He was a local biblical scholar and the president of the Association of Baptists for World Evangelism.

"This was a life-changing experience for all of us," Schmidt said. "We took turns hosting the study group at one another's homes, where we studied practical applications of the Bible, learned about the power of prayer, and shared in each other's search for spiritual truth."

On January 9, 1978, Schmidt dedicated his life to Christ. "I was convinced there was no other way to go through life than with a personal relationship with God, as laid out in the Bible," he said. "From that day of acceptance and rebirth, I have had a clear view of who's really in charge, of my relationship to Him, of the power and of that connection, and of the eternal hope that accompanies it."

Schmidt's decision to join the born-again movement was met with cynicism by the media and some teammates. There were a few players who questioned whether someone committed to Christ could bring a strong intensity to the field. Reporters chastised Baseball Chapel as a misguided use of religion and called team chaplains "good-luck charms." Schmidt had no idea that this spiritual movement would breed so much hostility and criticism. It further increased the scrutiny placed on him by everyone in Philadelphia.

* * *

Schmidt's spiritual revival made him feel like a new man. When he showed up for spring training in 1978, he was determined to have his best season and believed that his faith would help him get through the tough times. Danny Ozark reinforced Schmidt's optimism by naming him team captain before the season. Schmidt was not going to wear a "C" on his uniform like the captains do in the National Hockey League, but he was honored by the gesture.

"It's really something to think the players on the ballclub respect me enough to prefer me for this job," he said. "I don't think it's going to be any real big deal. I'm not going to be any different as a person than I am right now. This team doesn't need a guy to dive into bases like Pete Rose to turn it on. I'll lead by what I do on the field. If it still appears that I'm nonchalant out there, well, that's the way I am on the field."

The Phillies had won 101 games in consecutive seasons, but only had one playoff victory to show for it. All their important players were back and the Phillies again were favorites to win their division, and Schmidt came out swinging. By early May, he was batting .341 to lead the Phillies into first place. But Schmidt slumped badly the rest of the month and, not coincidentally, the Phillies dropped to third in the division. Schmidt continued his struggles in June, but Luzinski, Maddox, Bowa, and Bake McBride picked up the slack offensively. Philadelphia had moved into first place by late June when Schmidt suffered a badly pulled hamstring. He got five at-bats over a three-week span, finally returning to the lineup in mid-July. When he came back, his stroke was off and he looked a little clumsy at the plate. The strikeouts piled up, and fans booed Schmidt every chance they could get.

"The fans are trying to stimulate Mike," Ozark said. "They figure maybe he'll get mad and hit better. I don't think they're saying he's no good. They're just trying to stimulate something."

Schmidt simply ignored the critics. "I've decided that I deserve to be booed. There's no question about it," he said. "If I had a 'boo' sign in my back pocket I would pull it out and help them. I just want the people to know I would be booing myself. About all I can do is go out there and swing my way out of it and hope the cream will come to the top."

The fans were not the only ones taking their shots at Schmidt that season. Writers increased their criticism, picking on him for playing without emotion and saying he was "too cool" to be a complete player. One columnist called Schmidt's method of overthinking "paralysis by analysis."

Bowa recalls times when Schmidt went out of his way to try to prove he was a great all-around player.

"Schmitty would do stuff sometimes that would make you shake your head," Bowa said. "We were playing in Chicago one time. The wind was blowing out like 50 fucking miles per hour. Before the game, he comes up and says to Danny [Ozark], 'Hey, how about you do some hit-and-runs with me today.' I'm going, 'Schmitty, what the fuck? Just fuckin' hit! All you have to do is flip one in the air and it's going in the seats.' But that's what he would do. He wanted to hit-and-run. He was dead serious about it. He wanted to show people he can do everything."

"He would do stuff like when I was hitting in the top of the lineup," Bowa continued, "he would say, 'Hey, let's do a sign when you're on where I drop a bunt and you keep running to third.' I'd say, 'Schmitty, you're the No. 3 hitter in our lineup. Just fucking hit.' But he wanted to show people he can do all of it. He can hit, run, do it all. But he would bring up that shit in stupid situations."

Bob Boone warned Schmidt about talking too much at times because it seemed to backfire on him. "He'd talk to a certain writer for hours about hitting, and I would be thinking, *Oh, just shut up*, because the writer would then mock him in the paper because of the year he was having," Boone said.

Schmidt said he deserved the booing, but inside it bothered him. He could not understand why people continued to question his work ethic.

"How do the fans get the idea that we're not trying hard enough?" he asked. "Somehow, sure as hell, they can tell you the last time I left a man on third, or I left a winning run on second. And that has nothing to do with trying. People want to equate failing with lack of drive. Too often, failing is caused by too *much* drive."

Perhaps Schmidt had too much on his mind when he suffered through an embarrassing moment against the Mets in a game on September 23. Schmidt stole second base successfully but thought umpire Terry Tata had called him out. So he got up and headed back to the dugout—only to be tagged out by the pitcher.

"I'm not in a twilight zone," Schmidt explained. "I'm a human being."

Though he was not contributing much on the field, Schmidt tried to help his team by being a leader. He called a clubhouse meeting during a series in San Francisco in early September as the Phillies were clinging to first place. His message was simple: do whatever it takes to help the team win.

"What we've got to do is concentrate on nothing but scoring runs," he told the players. "Think about any way you can get to first, think about any way you can get to home plate. Get your minds on nothing else."

Veteran catcher Tim McCarver called Schmidt's speech his "finest hour as a professional."

Shortly after that meeting, the Phillies won six straight games and increased their lead from a half-game to four. They went to Pittsburgh for a season-ending four-game series, needing one win to clinch the division. After losing the first two, the Phillies beat the Pirates 10–8 in the next-to-last game of the regular season. Schmidt had a sacrifice fly in the victory and got a much-needed day off in the finale to rest his aching body.

Schmidt played that season through several nagging injuries, including a pulled hamstring, a broken second toe on his left foot, and various knee and shoulder problems. It reflected in his final stats: a .251 average, 21 home runs, and 78 RBIs. Those were his least productive numbers since his rookie year. But the Phillies had another meeting with the Los Angeles Dodgers in the National League Championship Series, so Schmidt would have a chance to make up for it when it counted most.

The Dodgers won 95 games in the regular season, five more than the Phillies. They had the same core of players that beat Philadelphia in the NLCS a year earlier before losing to the New York Yankees in the World Series. The series opened at Veterans Stadium and Burt Hooton, shaking off the nightmares from Black Friday, was on the mound for the Dodgers. Neither Hooton nor Phillies starter Larry Christensen were effective, and Los Angeles won 9–5.

Schmidt, who was 0-for-3 in the opener, found himself in an unfamiliar spot in the lineup for Game 2. Ozark batted him leadoff against Tommy John, a practice he tried a few times earlier in the season to wake Schmidt out of his slump. Schmidt singled leading off the bottom of the first, one of just four hits John allowed in a 4–0 victory that sent the Dodgers home one win away from clinching the pennant.

In Game 3, Carlton helped the Phillies avoid a sweep by tossing a complete game in a 9–4 victory. Schmidt, back to sixth in the lineup, had a double in four at-bats. Schmidt led off again in Game 4 and started it off with a double. The Phillies loaded the bases with no outs but could not score. It proved costly. The game went into extra innings tied at 3–3. In the tenth, the normally reliable Garry Maddox dropped a line drive hit by Dusty Baker to keep the inning alive. Bill Russell followed with an RBI single to end the series and send the Phillies home empty-handed again.

It was a trying season for Schmidt, who endured more negativity from the fans than he ever had before. But all the boos, catcalls, and criticism were put in perspective when Schmidt and Donna welcomed their first child, Jessica Rae, a week before Christmas.

When Schmidt held his daughter in his arms for the first time, he came to an important realization. "I knew for certain that life wasn't about money or status or cars or even baseball stardom," he said. "It's about loving God, serving others; it's about families and husbands and wives loving and respecting one another; and it's about having kids to love and raise."

Schmidt became more involved in community service, initially starting with the Christian Children's Fund. He later joined the United Way, established the Mike Schmidt Foundation, and established a scholarship program for students in inner-city schools in Philadelphia.

CHAPTER 5

Charlie Hustle's Influence

"There are players who run faster or hit for higher averages or steal more bases, but [Schmidt] does everything. He's the best player in the game."
—Pete Rose

The Philadelphia Phillies had all the ingredients needed to win in the late 1970s except one. They had a potent offense, outstanding pitching, and a solid defense. Still, they failed in the playoffs three straight years. Phillies management pinpointed the problem as a lack of veteran leadership, specifically a player who had a World Series ring and knew what it takes to win it all.

Pete Rose was the answer. Rose was the spark plug for the Cincinnati Reds and on a team filled with future Hall of Fame players, Rose was the inspirational leader. He helped the Big Red Machine win consecutive World Series championships in 1975 and 1976 and was a perennial All-Star at multiple positions.

Rose batted .302 with a league-leading 51 doubles in the last year of his contract in 1978. The 37-year-old third baseman also had a 44-game hitting streak that season. Despite his age, he was pursued aggressively on the free-agent market. The Phillies, Kansas City Royals, Pittsburgh Pirates, and several other teams wanted Rose, who was going through a stormy period in his marriage that made the Reds think hard about bringing him back. Eventually, he turned down more money from another team to sign with the Phillies because he liked their group of players and they offered a better chance for him to return to the World Series. The Phillies gave Rose a four-year, $3.2 million contract that temporarily made him the highest-paid athlete in team sports.

"I want to bring the world championship to a town that hasn't won it in half a century," Rose said. "If I can get the Phillies to win the World Series, I can do anything."

Nicknamed "Charlie Hustle" for his hard-nosed, all-out style, the switch-hitting Rose was known for his headfirst dives, batting out of a crouched stance, and running—instead of jogging—to first base whenever he walked. A native of Cincinnati, Rose broke into the major leagues as a second baseman with his hometown team in 1963. He was the National League Rookie of the Year that season and became an All-Star two years later. Rose helped the Reds win the NL pennant in 1970 and 1972 and was the NL's Most Valuable Player in 1973. He was MVP of the World Series in 1975 when the Reds beat the Boston Red Sox in seven games.

Growing up in Ohio, a young Mike Schmidt rooted for the Reds, and Pete Rose was one of his childhood heroes. His grandmother had a poster of Rose on the back of her bedroom door, and she used to tailor Schmidt's high school uniforms to fit snuggly the way Rose wore his. Rose's uncle, Buddy Bloebaum, was a scout for the Reds, and he gave Schmidt pointers on switch-hitting during his high school years. Now Schmidt would get a chance to play on the same team with one of his idols.

After Rose signed with the Phillies, there was quite a bit of speculation about where he would play. The Phillies already had an All-Star and Gold Glove winner playing third base for them. Rose quickly squelched rumors that Schmidt would move to second base. Some thought first baseman Richie Hebner would move to second and Rose would take first. Danny Ozark finally ended the talk.

"Pete Rose will be my first baseman in 1979 and hopefully for three years after that," Ozark said.

Rose had no problem trying out yet another position.

"All you have to do is catch the ball," he said. "They tell me the toughest thing is catching high pop-ups. I catch them in my hip pocket."

The signing of Rose was viewed as a sign that Philadelphia's front office thought the underachieving Phillies needed more leadership. Schmidt disagreed with that notion.

"That's ridiculous and it isn't fair to Pete to expect that sort of thing," Schmidt said. "When a team doesn't live up to expectations, it's natural to expect changes. This is simply one of those changes."

Years later, Schmidt looked back on the move and had a different opinion.

"The team needed an emotional leader, like Dave Cash in the early 1970s," Schmidt said. "We needed a guy we all respected, a guy who offered a different perspective, someone from another team who was a blue-chip player. Great teams have leaders at the top of the order who understand how valuable getting on base is, and no one understands this better than Pete."

Rose took some of the pressure off Schmidt, and his presence reduced the attention on the rest of the team. Once the Phillies signed Rose, all the talk around town was about him instead of the team's playoff failures. Rose took a special interest in Schmidt right away, and the two formed a close relationship that has lasted well beyond their playing careers.

By the time Rose arrived in Philadelphia, Schmidt had already established himself as a star player. He had won three home-run titles, played in three All-Star Games, and earned three Gold Glove Awards. But Rose saw more potential in Schmidt and wanted him to live up to it.

Rose and Schmidt were polar opposites on the field. While Schmidt was reserved and unemotional, Rose was an outgoing personality who played with high energy and intensity. Rose found different ways to make the game fun for Schmidt, helping him relax and enjoy his success. He nicknamed Schmidt "Herbie Lee" after a friend by that name whom Schmidt resembled. He helped Schmidt realize that acting serious all the time was not the only way to have success on the field. Rose joked around with Schmidt and other players often and did whatever he could to lighten the mood before games. Larry Bowa recalled the first time Rose noticed that Schmidt had a problem with sweating.

"Mike had a tendency to perspire big-time under his armpits before a game and he'd get ripped by his teammates," Bowa said. "I remember when Pete first came over, he saw this and he said, 'Schmitty, what the fuck? What are you sweating for?' And Schmitty said, 'I always get nervous before a game.' Pete said, 'You're nervous. How do you think that guy pitching against you tonight is gonna feel facing you in the batter's box? He must be fucking drenched with sweat.' He would say shit like that and Mike finally realized the pitcher should be scared of *him*."

Rose constantly boosted Schmidt's confidence, reminding him how great he could be and encouraging him when he was slumping. If Schmidt was going through a rough patch, Rose defended him in the press.

"Mike is human," Rose said. "He slumps like anybody else. One time he was slumping pretty bad and I thought he was carrying that onto the field, not giving 100 percent at third base. I offered him a little advice: 'When you're not hitting, that's the time to work extra hard on fielding. You're doing nothing with the bat, but you still contribute with the glove.'"

Rose never let Schmidt become complacent. He did not think any player should be satisfied with his accomplishments when he had the ability to do even more. If Rose got three hits in a game in his first three at-bats, he wanted to go 4-for-4, whereas most other players would be happy they already had three hits.

"Schmitty recognized he was gonna be a great player, but like Pete says, and I do believe this: Pete convinced him he could be a great player seven days a week, not just five days," Dallas Green said.

Rose was the consummate teammate. He was the first player to show up to the ballpark, and he would sit in the clubhouse and talk baseball for hours. He slapped hands with everyone, kept people thinking positively, and challenged others to play as hard as he did. Rose was the prototypical leadoff hitter, too. He took pitches, worked the count, drew walks, got a ton of hits, and consistently found ways to get on base so the sluggers behind him could drive him in. Rose would even sacrifice an at-bat to benefit other hitters.

"One time we were playing in New York and a rookie pitcher nobody ever heard of is going for the Mets," Bowa said. "Mike hated facing guys he never faced before. Couldn't stand it. He would rather face J.R. Richard or somebody he knew well. So he's sitting there at his locker and he's in one of those moods again, and Pete says, 'What's up?' Schmitty answers, 'I don't know this guy tonight. I don't know what he throws. I don't wanna face him.' Pete says, 'Tell you what, I'm leading off. I'll go up there and I'll show you 15 pitches and you're gonna see everything he has.' And I swear to God, Rose goes up there in the first inning and he's fouling off pitch after pitch, and he must've fouled off 10 to 15 before he makes an out. He comes back to the dugout and he says to Schmitty, 'Did you see the repertoire of pitches? He threw every pitch. Now go out and do some damage.'"

"There's no doubt about it. Pete Rose had a tremendous influence on my career," Schmidt said. "He made a major difference for me and for the Phillies. You have to remember that from 1976 to 1978 our team captured the National League East title each season, but nothing seemed to go right for us in the playoffs. I'm not sure we knew how to win in that five-game postseason series, and it didn't matter that you won 100 games during the regular season—if you couldn't win the playoffs, you were labeled a loser. The Phillies lived with that label until Pete Rose showed up."

With Pete Rose on board, the Phillies were eager to start the 1979 season and chase that elusive first World Series title. Anything less would be unacceptable in a city that desperately wanted a baseball championship.

General manager Paul Owens made another important move in spring training, acquiring second baseman Manny Trillo and pinch-hitting specialist Greg Gross from the Chicago Cubs in an eight-player deal. Trillo was an All-Star in 1977 and was known for his excellent defensive skills. Rose and Trillo gave the Phillies a new look on the right side of the infield, replacing Richie Hebner and Ted Sizemore. With Schmidt and Bowa anchoring the left side, the Phillies had arguably the best infield in the majors.

Coming off his worst season since his rookie year, Schmidt was anxious to put 1978 behind him. He hit four homers in the first nine games and was hitting close to .300 until a brief slump in late April dropped his average to .246. The Phillies went 14–5 in the first month and played even better in early May. Schmidt carried the offense, hitting five homers in one four-game stretch and five more in another four-game span. Then on May 17, the Phillies and Cubs played another one of those memorable games at Wrigley Field.

Schmidt and Bob Boone hit three-run homers and starting pitcher Randy Lerch added a solo shot to give the Phillies a 7–0 lead in the first inning. But no lead is ever safe at Wrigley, and the Cubs scored six runs in the bottom half of the first. An eight-run explosion in the top of the third and two more runs in the fourth put Philadelphia ahead 17–6. Once again, the Cubs answered with three in the fourth, seven in the fifth, and three in the sixth. Both teams continued trading runs, and the game was tied 22–22 after eight innings.

Cubs manager Herman Franks called on his best reliever, Bruce Sutter, to pitch the ninth and tenth. Sutter would end up winning the Cy Young

Award that season after saving 37 games. He pitched a scoreless ninth and retired the first two batters in the tenth before Schmidt stepped up to the plate. Schmidt worked a full count and Sutter threw his out pitch, a split-fingered fastball. It never sank. Schmidt blasted it into the left-field bleachers for his second home run of the game. Sutter did not even turn around to watch the ball; he knew it was gone right off the bat. Rawly Eastwick pitched a perfect tenth and the Phillies held on for a 23–22 victory in one of the wildest games in baseball history.

The 45 runs scored were four short of the major league record set 57 years earlier when the Cubs beat the Phillies 26–23 (at Wrigley Field, of course). The game featured 11 home runs, including three by Cubs slugger Dave Kingman, and 50 hits. It certainly helped that there was a stiff wind blowing out to left field.

The Phillies improved to 24–10 with the victory and held a 3½-game lead over the Montreal Expos for first place in the division. They had just completed a 14-game road trip and were heading home to play their next 10 games. Everything seemed to be going right for the Phillies. But then the Expos came into Veterans Stadium and swept a three-game series, sending the Phillies into a major free fall. They lost 12 of their next 15 games and dropped to third place.

By July 1, the Phillies had plummeted to fifth place and were 7½ games out of first. But they quickly turned things around and closed within three games of the division-leading Expos by the All-Star break. Schmidt had an incredible first half; rebounding from his dismal 1978 season, he clubbed 31 homers and was on pace to challenge Roger Maris' single-season home-run record of 61 set in 1961.

Schmidt homered in four straight at-bats over two games against the San Francisco Giants in early July. He connected off Gary Lavelle in the final at-bat of a 6–1 win, and the next night he took John Montefusco deep twice and homered off Pedro Borbon in his first three at-bats.

"I remember I just missed hitting a fifth off Borbon," Schmidt said. "Hit it to the warning track."

Midway through the season, Schmidt made a major adjustment to his batting stance. He moved deeper in the batter's box and farther away from the plate, the same way Pittsburgh Pirates outfielder Roberto Clemente used to hit. The change allowed Schmidt to hit for more power to the opposite field while helping him become a better all-around hitter. Schmidt tried out his new stance in the All-Star Game and ripped an RBI triple off California Angels flamethrower Nolan Ryan in the first inning. He also hit a double later in the game, helping the National League stars to a 7–6 win.

"I wanted a stance that gave me a strike zone like Pete Rose's and that produced balls hit in Clemente-fashion with power to all fields," Schmidt said.

Schmidt's new stance allowed him to stride toward the plate instead of toward the pitcher. That forced him to take his left shoulder into the ball instead of opening up, and it helped him hit more balls to the gaps and right field instead of down the left-field line. He no longer was a dead-pull hitter because he could spray the ball anywhere on the field. Moving off the plate also made Schmidt less vulnerable to inside pitches and prevented him from getting jammed. He was able to wait longer on pitches because he was farther back in the box.

"Changing my position in the batter's box is more complicated than experimenting with different bats," Schmidt said. "Where and how you stand affects your whole style of hitting. I made a conscious change in my style that was as much mental as physical, one that helped me become the kind of hitter I knew I could be."

After the short break, the Phillies resorted to their losing ways and they dropped eight of the first 10 games. They had losing streaks of six, four, and five games in August, and fell below .500 and completely out of contention. Injuries took a toll on the team. Trillo missed over a month with a broken arm; Boone, Bowa, and Greg Luzinski also were sidelined for significant periods. Still, management refused to make excuses for the team's poor performance and Paul Owens decided a drastic change was needed. He fired Danny Ozark on August 31 and replaced him with farm director Dallas Green. The two men were complete opposites. While Ozark was laid-back and soft-spoken, Green was loud, brash, and had a volatile temper.

Green pitched in parts of eight seasons in the major leagues with the Phillies, Washington Senators, and New York Mets, compiling a 20–22 record. He joined Philadelphia's front office after retiring in 1967, serving first as assistant director of the minor leagues and later as the head of the farm system. When Green moved into the dugout, players were not happy about the switch.

"We had a constant battle about how I wanted the game played and how I wanted the team to go about their business," Green said. "It started because Danny got fired and they loved Danny. He was a good baseball guy and he was a perfect guy for our team growing up, but he let them run the team. Pope [Owens] and I talked about it and that's not how we wanted it done anymore. The guys had a hell of a time understanding the game plan was the game plan and I wasn't going to let them deviate. That was my job. It was kind of our last hurrah. I had to convince them to play team baseball and there's a way to go about it and not to sit back and wait for Schmitty and Bull to hit three-run homers."

Green, a big man with a resounding voice, immediately stirred things up when he said he would use the final month of the season to evaluate the team and see who wanted to play. He yelled at players, criticized them in the press, and made it clear they either played the game his way or they would be sent packing. The Phillies responded on the field, winning 19 of their last 30 games to finish in fourth place at 84–78.

Green and Schmidt had many differences in opinion early in their relationship. Green was a stickler for fundamentals and he had no tolerance for any player he perceived to be lackadaisical. The new manager changed several rules in the clubhouse, including one that limited the time players could play cards. Many players would pass the time by playing cards until the game started; Green made them stop once batting practice started before home games. For away games, they had to stop playing cards approximately two hours before the first pitch. Green also instituted a dress code for road trips, leaving it up to Schmidt, who preferred casual clothes, to decide which type of jeans would be acceptable. One of Green's toughest rules was making the team take infield practice before games, a practice that has been abandoned by managers nowadays. Schmidt did not care for it much back then, which led to some conflicts with Green.

"I made him take infield every day, and he hated that with a passion," Green said. "But I made him do it every day and I said, 'You're gonna do it unless you're hurt or you come to me and say you need a day off.' I said, 'Schmitty, it's not punishment or necessarily a preparation for the game. It's a mental preparation, not a physical preparation. Just go out there and take grounders, throw to first, and turn double plays.' What it does is click in your mind that you only have 20 more minutes until the game. It's a mental thing that tells you that you only have so much time until the game. Otherwise, if you don't take infield, you sit in the goddamn clubhouse and you are doing nothing for an hour and a half."

Schmidt would have rather spent that time working on his hitting. Many veterans let backup players take infield for them. Green allowed them to continue doing that, but fined them $100 each time with the money going to charity.

"If I'm in a slump, I'll come out early," Schmidt said. "I want some extra batting practice, either in the batting cage in the tunnel or on the field. Besides, I like to get to the ballpark early because I don't like to hurry doing anything. I want to take my time. If I need to get in the whirlpool to soak my muscles, I want to be able to do that."

Schmidt always was an early arrival to the ballpark, getting there around 3:00 PM for games that started at 7:30 PM. He worked hard, but he preferred doing things *his* way. He took his grounders while pitchers had their batting practice instead of with the rest of the infielders.

Schmidt begrudgingly agreed to do things Green's way, and took out his frustrations on pitchers. He finished the 1979 season with 45 homers, far short of Maris' mark. But it was a tremendous improvement from the 18 he hit the year before. Schmidt batted .253 and drove in 114 runs.

Rose hit .331 in his first season in Philadelphia, living up to high expectations with his new team. But 1979 was a tough year for Rose off the field. First, a woman filed a paternity suit against him, alleging he fathered her 10-month-old daughter. Later in the summer, Rose's reputation took another hit following an interview with *Playboy* magazine.

Rose admitted he took "greenies," which are amphetamine pills legal only by prescription. He also made a racial comment when asked why he got so many endorsements.

"Look, if you owned Swanson's Pizza, would you want a black guy to do the commercial on TV for you? Would you like the black guy to pick up the pizza and bite into it? Or would you want Pete Rose?" Rose said.

The Campbell Soup Company, which owned Swanson Pizza, quickly disassociated itself from Rose and reminded customers it had used black athletes Roosevelt Grier and Ed "Too Tall" Jones to endorse its products.

"*Playboy* made me lose my cool," Rose later said. "There it is. I was bad."

Rose's turbulent year culminated with his wife Karolyn filing for divorce in September. Rose did not contest the divorce, though it took a while for the property settlement.

Despite Rose's off-the-field problems, he was a clubhouse leader and he was clearly instrumental in Schmidt's resurgence. Rose was very impressed with his new teammate.

"There are players who run faster or hit for higher averages or steal more bases, but he does everything," Rose said of Schmidt. "He's the best player in the game."

But the best player still had no ring, the true measure for a superstar.

"No one can really say what makes a successful player," Schmidt said. "That fragile combination of skill, attitude, and circumstance is different for each one. But there are certain qualities that successful players share—qualities that make it possible for them to be there in the end, that let their talent come through in clutch situations, when the most is demanded of a player. That's what it means to play baseball in October.

"Superior skill alone doesn't make a successful player. It's using what skills you have and getting the most out of them—performing to your capacity and then some when it counts the most. For those players with exceptional ability, how well they use it when it counts the most will determine if they move into the ranks of the all-time great players. World

Series baseball for me, as for many others, seemed to be the missing ingredient for top-player status."

While Rose was in Philadelphia, Schmidt and other players were aware that he enjoyed gambling. They would sit around the clubhouse and discuss point spreads for football and basketball games. But no one realized the depth of Rose's problem until several years later.

In 1989, reports surfaced that Rose had bet on baseball games while he was managing the Reds, a position he had held since 1984. Rose strongly denied those allegations, but he voluntarily accepted a place on baseball's ineligible list on August 24, 1989. According to the rules, Rose would be allowed to apply for reinstatement in one year. Twenty years later, he still remains on the banned list. The situation bothers Schmidt, who has tried many times to help Rose smooth things over with Major League Baseball.

"Pete's banishment has weighed very heavily on him and his family," Schmidt said. "He has had immense financial problems triggered by a free-fall drop in income as a result of the ban. He has had major problems with the IRS. And he has had to carry a crippling burden of guilt. Pete's life was baseball, and to be forbidden to be involved with any aspect of it was for him the equivalent of pure torture."

Over the years, Rose has gained tremendous support from fans, former teammates, and some members of the media who think he served his punishment and deserves to be allowed back in baseball. Many feel baseball's all-time hits leader certainly belongs in the Hall of Fame, and Schmidt has been Rose's biggest ally. In 2002, baseball commissioner Bud Selig agreed to meet with Rose, and he asked Schmidt to serve as a liaison between him and the banned superstar. Schmidt was honored to have a chance to help Rose make amends.

"Like just about everybody else who knew Pete, I wanted to believe his story, and I always gave him the benefit of the doubt publicly," Schmidt said. "But knowing Pete's penchant for gambling and his habit of hanging out with sleazy people, it wasn't hard for me to see the other side as a potential reality. But before I could go to bat for Pete, I had to know that he was going to be totally honest and forthright with me regarding baseball and gambling. I would not put my own reputation in jeopardy in support of anything shady or duplicitous, as we were moving headlong into a national media explosion and I would be smack in the middle. I also believed Pete needed the help of a close friend, someone he respected, someone who wanted only the best for him, someone who wasn't looking to take advantage of him."

Rose came across as cocky and arrogant when he was a player, and his reputation had been smeared because of his gambling issues and legal problems that landed him a five-month jail sentence in 1990. But Schmidt knew a different side of Rose.

"I believed Pete to have a gigantic heart, always willing to give of himself to those around him," Schmidt said. "I knew he had always been lacking, mostly of his own doing, a personal life of love and friendship. I thought this might put him in a more human light, not only with the commissioner and with the fans, but with his family."

Schmidt met with Rose and his adviser, Warren Greene, for breakfast on November 25, 2002. He asked Rose if he was ready to make things right and admit that he had bet on baseball. Rose replied, "Herbie, I can't go any longer."

The trio then headed for the meeting with Selig at the commissioner's office in Milwaukee, Wisconsin. After some casual conversation, Selig asked if he could speak privately with Rose. Schmidt was not in the room when Rose confessed that he bet on baseball while he was the Reds' manager. In Rose's mind, he did his part. But Selig was not convinced.

"I spoke to Bud later, and he told me he got the confession he had expected but not the expression of genuine remorse he had hoped for," Schmidt said. "At the time, though, the meeting seemed to be a success. We thought a positive response from the commissioner was a lock. We thought Pete was going to be accepted back by baseball. We thought he was going to be allowed to come home."

Instead, Rose got no response from Selig. In January 2004, Rose released his second autobiography, called *My Prison Without Bars*, in which he admitted to betting on baseball. The timing of the book rankled baseball officials because it came out the same week the Hall of Fame class was announced. It also seemed to seal Rose's fate because he is still waiting for a response from Selig.

"It wasn't the best showing of sorrow and regret," Schmidt said a month after the book hit stores. "That's just something Pete isn't great at doing. But I know that he truly is sorry and that he regrets everything. He talked to me in private about it, told me that he let me down. And he broke down.

"As soon as I got off the phone with him, I contacted the commissioner and told him, 'This guy means what he's saying.' I believe in him, and I don't want to get caught in a con game. Pete's a beaten man."

Rose's eligibility to appear on the ballot for the Hall of Fame voting expired in 2006. Schmidt firmly believes Rose belongs in the Hall.

"To me, Pete Rose and baseball are inseparable," Schmidt said. "Pete bet on baseball. He bet on his own team to win. Against baseball law? Absolutely. So heinous a crime that it must never be forgiven? Not in my book. Had Pete thrown games or ever played to lose, we wouldn't be having a conversation. But Peter Edward Rose Sr. never played to lose at anything. He played in more winning games than any player in history. He was a winner. What he did was bad. But not bad enough to banish him from baseball forever."

CHAPTER 6

A Dream Season

*"My big moment, my chance to erase all
the doubts back in Philly that I'm a money player.
Instead, I strike out, and I got in search of the
nearest hole to crawl into."*

—Mike Schmidt

Paul Owens, Dallas Green, and other members of the Phillies' front office had to make a crucial decision in the winter of 1979. The Phillies were coming off a fourth-place finish after winning three straight division titles and failing in the playoffs each year. They had a nucleus of players that had been together for the better part of the decade. Management had to decide if the team had gone as far as it could with the current group; if so, they would break up the core of the Phillies. If not, they would keep them together and take one more run at a championship before making any major changes.

Green, who was originally supposed to return to the front office after spending the final month of the 1979 season as the team's manager, decided he wanted a full year in the dugout to see if he could make a difference. Owens convinced ownership to give it one more try before dismantling the team. The roster was in place. There were no key trades or big-name free-agent signings in the off-season. The Phillies had to win with the players they already had or everyone could become expendable. There were several young players in the minor league system that deserved a promotion and could get a chance to play, especially if a veteran slumped or had a poor season.

"That was the reason I was out there, because if we didn't win, Pope [Owens] was gonna change everything because we had been getting a little long in the tooth and guys had been there for a long time," Green said.

Mike Schmidt was 30 years old at that point, and he certainly had matured as a ballplayer and a person. Under Danny Ozark, he was the team captain. Once Green took over as manager, Schmidt was uncertain what his role might be. With Pete Rose on the team, he felt a little awkward about being the captain. Rose was almost 10 years older than Schmidt, he had two World Series rings, and was assumed to be a certain future Hall of Famer. Schmidt asked Green after he replaced Ozark if he could resign as captain and pass the duties to Rose. Green told him he would think about it over the winter. When the team reconvened for spring training, there was no captain.

"We don't have a captain because we don't need a captain," Green said. "What can a captain do besides take the lineup card out to home plate? With my open-door policy, I don't need a go-between. A player has every right to come in at any time and say, 'Skip, can I have a few minutes?' If you're gonna lay the authority figure on them or play God, you're gonna back some people off. I don't see the need for a captain on a veteran club, other than Pete Rose, and Pete doesn't want the responsibility."

That first spring under Green was intense. His booming voice was the loudest sound heard every morning at the team's practice complex. Green made sure the dismal finish the previous year was fresh in the mind of every player. He reminded them of their failures and let them know it would be unacceptable to fall short again. Green held long workouts stressing the fundamentals, which normally is more important for younger teams, not a veteran club like the Phillies. Many players had a problem accepting Green's tough-love approach, including Schmidt.

"I don't know if Dallas' screaming is all that significant," Schmidt said. "What is significant is that we're working harder and we're getting more accomplished. We'll execute better. We won't give as many games away. If he screams at me, more than likely, I'll deserve it. Besides, it doesn't hurt to get kicked in the rear end once in a while. It might just make me a better ballplayer."

Green felt that Schmidt understood where he was coming from, but the Phillies' slugger did not have the type of personality to stand up and proclaim his support for the manager.

"Schmitty all along wanted to buy into it, but there was always a reluctance because of the respect he had for Danny Ozark and the team," Green said. "He got along with all the guys probably except for Bo [Larry Bowa]. It wasn't an outright defiance, but there was an undertone of, 'Ah, we're not sure you know what the hell you're doing' and 'We've been in it in '76, '77, '78, and we know what we're doing.' I tried to get that eliminated. Pete Rose and [Steve] Carlton helped me with that considerably.

"I said, 'You went to the dance but you didn't dance with anybody.' You always sensed Schmitty wanted to win, but he always wanted to do it the old way or his way. The infield thing stuck in his craw and the way I treated players, my screaming and yelling and my usual bullshit, stuck in his craw. He was never surly or disrespectful, but there was a sense of reluctance to say, 'Okay, D, you're on the right track and we'll kick in here.' He was fighting the infield thing and fighting this and fighting that, saying, 'I wish he didn't talk to the media' and 'I wish he didn't do this' or 'I wish he didn't do that.'"

A players' strike canceled the final week of spring training. The Phillies had no problem with that, considering it meant one less week dealing with Green. But when the Phillies headed north to start the season, they were not ready to play. Maybe that extra week of practice would have helped. After winning the first two games, they lost nine of the next 13. A combination of poor hitting and inconsistent pitching in April put the Phillies in trouble early in the season. Except for Schmidt and Bob Boone, the rest of the lineup struggled. Even Rose had a rough start, batting .226 the first month.

But things turned around in May with Schmidt leading the way. He hit two homers in a 7–1 victory over Atlanta on May 5 that evened the Phillies record at 10–10. At that point, Schmidt had eight home runs and 18 RBIs in 20 games. He had another two-homer game in a 7–0 win over the Chicago Cubs at Wrigley Field on the final day of the month as the Phillies went 17–9 in May and closed within one game of the division-leading Pittsburgh Pirates, who were the defending World Series champions.

Two months into the season, Schmidt was batting .301 with 16 homers and 41 RBIs. It looked like Rose's prediction in spring training that Schmidt would be the National League's Most Valuable Player was right on. Rose played with three former MVPs in Cincinnati—Joe Morgan, Johnny Bench, and George Foster—so he knew Schmidt had the potential and kept reminding him that he did.

"We've developed a tremendous professional rapport, and I've grown as a ballplayer through this relationship," Schmidt said of his friendship with Rose. "We understand each other well, and I know Pete has a great respect for my ability to play the game. He always shows me how much he wants me to succeed. I also know he enjoys watching me play because he always tells me so. That's a great positive reinforcement coming from a living legend like Pete, and I try to return the respect he shows me."

The Phillies stumbled a bit in June and July, going 29–28 over those two months. Schmidt slumped, too. His average dropped to .269 and he had just 11 homers in those two months. Still, Schmidt was the leading vote-getter for the All-Star Game and he made his fifth trip to the Midsummer Classic. Carlton and Rose joined him for the game played at Dodger Stadium in Los Angeles. Schmidt did not play because of a pulled hamstring, however.

The team's problems on the field took a back seat to other issues. A week before the All-Star Game, Schmidt, Rose, Larry Bowa, and Greg Luzinski were named in a newspaper story that said Pennsylvania authorities wanted to question "at least eight members of the Phillies about allegedly acquiring amphetamine pills illegally" from a doctor in Reading, Pennsylvania. Amphetamines are diet pills known as "greenies" that many players took as stimulants during that era. Schmidt and Rose immediately denied the allegations, but they were still asked to testify in court. Owens denied knowledge of the investigation until the report broke in the *Trenton (New Jersey) Times* on July 8. Team vice president Bill Giles called the report "irresponsible journalism."

Phillies owner Ruly Carpenter held a news conference four days after learning about the report. Carpenter insisted that none of his players had "broken any laws" and called the allegations "speculative." The fallout from the story and the negative publicity left players bitter toward the media. Bowa refused to speak to reporters, and Schmidt was upset that reporters took "the liberty to tarnish" his name. Years later, Schmidt admitted the Phillies were not exactly innocent in the whole situation.

"In my day, amphetamines were widely available in major league clubhouses," he said. "They were obtainable with a prescription, but be under no illusion that the name on the bottle always coincided with the name of the player taking them before games."

While the drug scandal played out, Rose's divorce proceedings took center stage that summer. His wife Karolyn took her story to the national press, painting an unflattering picture of Rose as a husband. Rose somehow managed to ignore the problems at home and do his job when he came to the ballpark.

All the negative issues off the field seemed to overshadow the team's poor performance. A six-game losing streak in late July dropped the Phillies into third place. Green was still fuming when the Phillies returned home after losing three straight in Atlanta and three more in Cincinnati.

"All I can do is scream and yell and kick and holler," he said. "You still go back to character. That's what makes a ballclub. But we've told them that a thousand times."

Green's comments infuriated Luzinski, who was on the disabled list with a knee injury. He blasted the manager before a home game against the Reds.

"I think he's hurting us," Luzinski said, nodding in the direction of Green's office. "He's trying to be a fucking gestapo. I read his quotes in the newspaper, and it really pisses me off."

Sensing his reaction might get a lot of attention, the left fielder backtracked a bit. "Don't get me wrong," Luzinski said. "I like playing for the guy; it's just some of the things he says about character affects some of the guys. They're sensitive guys who are getting singled out for one bad pitch or one bad play."

Luzinski then pointed to the sign that was hanging above the clubhouse door and ripped his manager some more.

"That sign says, 'We, Not I.' It should go both ways," he continued. "But he says 'we' when we win, and he says 'they' when we lose. The thing is, and Dallas has said this himself, he's got shortcomings and one of them is his mouth."

Luzinski was not the only player who had issues with Green. Bowa feuded with him publicly, and Schmidt took exception with Green's ranting and raving and the way he treated some players. Green benched Luzinski, Boone, and Garry Maddox and refused to pitch Larry Christensen at various points during the season. Schmidt was very close with Maddox, so he stepped in whenever he thought Green was mistreating him.

"He and Maddox were buddies. I got crossways with Maddox a couple times and [Schmidt] would always try to be protective of Garry and he would come in and talk to me and I tried to explain where I was headed and where I was going," Green said.

Schmidt would have preferred if Green kept team issues more private rather than address things in public through the media. "Every day you would walk into the clubhouse and wonder what was waiting for you," Schmidt said. "Who said who was a gutless jerk? Who said who was lazy? Or who was selfish? It was like a soap opera. There was a feeling among the players that this wasn't the way to do things. If you were going to preach togetherness, then you'd better practice it. If you had a problem with a player, call him in and read him the riot act behind closed doors. Don't take every dispute public."

The whole team was not against Green; he had his supporters. Veteran reliever Sparky Lyle, acquired as insurance after closer Tug McGraw went on the disabled list, understood Green's agenda. Infielder John Vukovich was perhaps the strongest Green loyalist. Rookies Lonnie Smith, Keith Moreland, and Bob Walk also liked Green because he gave them a chance to play. Besides, the youngsters already knew Green's gruff personality from their years playing under him in the minor leagues, so they were used to his antics by the time they finally reached the big club.

Owner Ruly Carpenter downplayed the tension in the clubhouse. "A third of the players are going to like the manager. Another third aren't going to like him, and the job of the owner is to keep the third that's undecided from joining the mutiny," Carpenter said. "I couldn't have cared less what the players thought. If they had a difference with Dallas, they'd straighten it out with him. It wasn't my responsibility."

An 8–4 homestand helped the Phillies pull within three games of the first-place Montreal Expos going into an important four-game series against the Pirates at Three Rivers Stadium in early August. Schmidt called a players-only meeting before the series to make sure everyone understood the magnitude of the upcoming games.

"The message was, we had to step up and play better," Green said. "Well, we played terrible instead."

The Phillies lost the first two games and then dropped the opener of a Sunday doubleheader. By then, Green had seen enough. Between games, he went off on the players in an infamous clubhouse tirade that *Philadelphia Daily News* baseball writer Bill Conlin heard through the steel doors.

"This game isn't easy. It's fucking tough, and we're fucking hurting with injuries," Green screamed. "But you fucking guys got your fucking heads down. You got to stop being so fucking cool. If you don't get that through your fucking heads, you're gonna be so fucking buried it ain't gonna be fucking funny. Get the fuck up off your butts and go beat somebody. You're a fucking good baseball team. But you're not now. You can't look in the fucking mirror. You keep telling me you can do it, but you fucking give up. If you don't want to play, get the fuck in that office and tell me, 'I don't want to fucking play anymore.' Because if you feel that way, I don't want to play you."

Though it seemed harsh at the time, that memorable speech was exactly what the Phillies needed to get things turned around. They lost the second game of the doubleheader to the Pirates to fall six games out of first, but a trip to Chicago helped the Phillies get back on track. They won eight of their next nine games and inched closer to first place. Schmidt had another big series at Wrigley Field. He homered in three straight games and went 8-for-14. He made it four consecutive games with a homer and added three more hits in a victory over the New York Mets. The Phillies were rolling, but they were not through getting reprimanded.

After a sloppy loss to the San Diego Padres in which center fielder Garry Maddox dropped two balls, it was Owens' turn to speak his mind. When the players arrived in San Francisco for the start of a three-game set against the Giants, the general manager was waiting for them.

"You guys played the first five months for yourselves. You've gone your own different ways. Your manager has been trying to get things across to you and now I'm telling you: stop your goddamned pouting!" Owens yelled. "I stuck my neck out after 1979 by refusing to break up this team. I wanted to give you guys another chance! Now it's my turn. The last month belongs to me and you had better deliver."

The Phillies responded to Owens' ultimatum by sweeping the Giants and moving into first place. Schmidt was only 3-for-13 in the series, but Philadelphia's pitchers were excellent. They held the Giants to eight runs in three games, which included a 2–1 victory in 13 innings in the middle game.

"Pope really got into them. From that day on, we played our asses off," Green said.

After San Francisco, the Phillies went to Los Angeles. They beat the Dodgers 3–2 in the series opener to move a game ahead of Montreal and Pittsburgh. Schmidt hit a two-run homer in the first inning off Jerry Reuss to get the offense started. But Los Angeles won the next three games. The Phillies and Expos went back and forth, exchanging first place several times over the final month until the last weekend of the season when the teams met at Olympic Stadium.

A week before that series, Schmidt experienced a personal tragedy. His grandmother, Viola Schmidt, passed away at age 78 following a battle with cancer. She died on September 26, a day before Schmidt's 31st birthday. The Phillies beat the Expos that night at the Vet to take a 1½-game lead in the standings. Schmidt homered on his birthday, but Montreal won 4–3. The Expos took the final game to move back into first place by a half-game.

Schmidt flew home to Dayton for the funeral on September 29, but returned in time to play against the Chicago Cubs. After the Cubs scored two runs to take a 5–3 lead in the top of the fifteenth inning, the Phillies rallied in the bottom half. They had cut the deficit to 5–4 and had a runner on third with one out when Schmidt came up to the plate. Dennis Lamp came in from the bullpen to face Schmidt, who was looking to hit a fly ball to drive in the tying run. Instead, he popped out to second base. But Maddox, who entered the game in the twelfth inning, followed with a game-tying single, and Manny Trillo singled home the winning run a few batters later.

Hoping to shake up the team, Green had benched three of his regulars—Greg Luzinski, Bob Boone, and Maddox—that night. He was relieved the move did not backfire. Schmidt was even more relieved because he failed in a clutch situation.

"That was the first time we really felt like things had come together for us as a team," Schmidt said. "In the past, it seemed that my teammates couldn't pick me up and the burden of failure would be even greater on me than anyone else in the same situation. But this time, Garry Maddox came off the bench to tie the game, and later, Manny Trillo won it. Those guys picking me up the way they did made it possible for me to do some of the things I did against the Cubs later in the series."

The Phillies won the next game 14–2. Schmidt broke a scoreless tie in the sixth inning with his 45th homer in a 5–0 victory the following night. He hit another homer as the Phillies completed the four-game sweep with a 4–2 victory in the series finale, setting up a final showdown in Montreal. After 159 games, the Phillies and Expos were tied for first place.

The Expos joined the league in 1969 and did not have a winning record until they finished in second place behind the Pirates in 1979. They had a roster that featured several young offensive stars including Gary Carter, Andre Dawson, Larry Parrish, and Ellis Valentine. Their pitching staff had a mix of veterans—ace Steve Rogers and closer Woodie Fryman—and youngsters—Scott Sanderson, Bill Gullickson, and David Palmer.

On the morning of the series opener, Schmidt woke up with flu-like symptoms. He was coughing, sneezing, and feeling achy, but he refused medicine because he did not want to risk any side effects. The game was delayed by rain for a few hours. When it started, Dick Ruthven outdueled Sanderson and the Phillies won 2–1. Schmidt drove in both runs with a sacrifice fly in the first inning and a homer in the sixth.

"Maybe it was better that I had the flu," Schmidt said. "I didn't get all tensed up like I usually do for big games. I didn't try to do something superhuman."

The Phillies' magic number for clinching the division was down to one. The game on Saturday afternoon was scheduled to be aired on NBC, but rain pushed the start time back three hours until 5:25 PM. Despite several baserunning blunders and five errors, the Phillies took a 3–2 lead into the bottom of the seventh inning. But Ron Reed and Sparky Lyle each allowed a run and the Expos went ahead 4–3.

Fryman came in for the save in the ninth. Pete Rose led off with a walk, but Bake McBride and Schmidt each grounded out. That brought up Boone, who did not start the game. He delivered a single to center that scored the tying run and sent the game into extra innings.

The game stayed tied until the eleventh inning. After Rose led off with a single, McBride popped out. Schmidt stepped in against Stan Bahnsen, the fourth pitcher used by Expos manager Dick Williams. Bahnsen fell behind in the count 2–0 and decided to challenge Schmidt with a fastball. Schmidt nailed it into the left-field seats to give the Phillies a 6–4 lead. Tug McGraw pitched a 1-2-3 inning to seal the win, and the Phillies clinched the National League East title for the fourth time in five years.

"That was as clutch a homer as he'd ever hit because of what it meant to the team," Green said of Schmidt's blast off Bahnsen.

The usually reserved Schmidt danced around the bases after his mighty drive, and he stomped his feet on home plate where he was greeted and hugged by his teammates.

"This is very meaningful to me," Schmidt said amid the champagne celebration. "Not many people thought we could come up here and take two of three from them in their own park. But we did it. I am deeply satisfied. Today, I made it happen. There's all the heart possible in this dressing room right now, but if we don't win in the playoffs, people will call us the same old Phillies."

Years later, Schmidt called that homer the "defining moment" of his career. "I needed that series," he said. "Philly fans were split on me, whether I was a money player. It hurt me to know they doubted me, but personally I doubted myself, too. I hadn't hit well in the postseason, and the fans hadn't forgotten it. I needed to step up. Fortunately, I did."

While the battle between the Expos and Phillies in the East came down to the next-to-last game, the National League West race went to overtime. The Houston Astros and Los Angeles Dodgers finished tied after 162 games because the Astros blew a three-game lead with three remaining by getting swept by the Dodgers. But the Astros beat the Dodgers 7–1 in a one-game playoff to advance to the National League Championship Series against the Phillies. Though this was basically the same group of players—except for Rose—that had lost three straight years in the NLCS, the Phillies had a different mental approach this time.

"It's the same bunch of guys who had had a great deal of adversity in common," Schmidt said before the series. "But this team has character. The way we're playing now, the team has proven to me it's ready to play the best teams in baseball."

Schmidt finished the regular season with a .286 average and career highs in homers (48) and RBIs (121). He won the Most Valuable Player Award, just as Rose predicted back in spring training. Personal goals were nice, but the ultimate goal was to win a World Series title.

"No matter how you perform individually, no matter how many home run titles you win, it means little if you're not part of a winning team," Schmidt said.

* * *

The Houston Astros entered the league as the Colt .45s in 1962. They had never reached the postseason until 1980. Before that, the Astros were mostly known for the building they played in: the Astrodome, the world's first domed stadium.

Nicknamed the "Eighth Wonder of the World," the Astrodome opened in 1965. It was a pitcher's paradise because of its cavernous power alleys. Terry Puhl led the Astros with 13 home runs in 1980, 35 fewer than Mike Schmidt hit for the Phillies. Over time, there were fewer homers hit at the Astrodome than any other ballpark in the league.

The Astros did not have to rely on the long ball to win games in 1980. They had an excellent lineup filled with solid hitters and good basestealers. Puhl (.282) and fellow outfielders Cesar Cedeno (.309) and Jose Cruz (.302) were the hitting stars along with first baseman

Art Howe (.283). Aging second baseman Joe Morgan provided veteran leadership. Six players stole more than 20 bases, with Cedeno's 48 swipes leading the team.

Joe Niekro (20–12, 3.55 ERA) was the ace of a staff that featured hard-throwing right-hander Nolan Ryan (11–10, 3.35) and 12-game winners Ken Forsch and Vern Ruhle. The Astros overcame the loss of J.R. Richard (10–4, 1.89) after he suffered a near-fatal stroke in July that eventually ended his career. Closer Joe Sambito (17 saves) anchored a deep bullpen.

The Phillies were led offensively by Schmidt, of course. Bake McBride (.309), Manny Trillo (.292), and Pete Rose (.282) also put up good numbers that season. Rookies Lonnie Smith (.339) and Keith Moreland (.314) played well in limited time. Smith appeared in 100 games, filling in often for outfielders Greg Luzinski (.228, 19 HR, 56 RBIs) and Garry Maddox (.259, 11 HR, 73 RBIs) because both had subpar years. Moreland stepped in for catcher Bob Boone, who hit just .229.

Steve Carlton led the pitching staff with 24 wins and a 2.34 ERA. Dick Ruthven (17–10, 3.55) was a solid No. 2 starter. Rookie Bob Walk won 11 games, and Marty Bystrom came up from the minors when rosters were expanded on September 1 and went 5–0 down the stretch. Larry Christensen was 5–1 in only 14 starts because of injuries, but he would be counted on to pitch in the playoffs.

The Phillies dominated Houston in the regular season, winning nine of the 12 meetings between the teams. The Astros had more overall wins (93–91), and since it was the Western Division champion's turn to have home-field advantage, the last three games of the NLCS would be in the Astrodome.

The series opened at Veterans Stadium in front of 65,277 rabid fans. Carlton outdueled Forsch and Luzinski hit a two-run homer to lead the Phillies to a 3–1 victory. It was their first win in a home playoff game since the opener of the 1915 World Series when Grover Cleveland Alexander beat the Boston Red Sox at the Baker Bowl.

Houston evened the series the next night with a 7–4 win in 10 innings. Ryan started for the Astros and allowed two runs in 6 ⅓ innings. Ruthven pitched well for the Phillies, giving up two runs in seven innings. But Philadelphia's bullpen struggled. Tug McGraw allowed a go-ahead run in the eighth and Ron Reed gave up four in the tenth after the Phillies tied it in the bottom of the eighth on Maddox's second RBI hit.

After a day off, the series moved to the Astrodome for Game 3. Christensen got the start for the Phillies against Niekro, who was a master of the knuckleball. Both pitchers were excellent. Christensen tossed six shutout innings while Niekro pitched 10 scoreless innings. Houston won it in the bottom of the eleventh off McGraw; Morgan started the inning with a triple, and Denny Walling hit a game-winning sacrifice fly after two intentional walks. The Astros had a 2–1 lead in the series and were one win away from their first trip to the World Series.

Facing elimination, the Phillies sent Carlton to the mound on three days' rest to face Ruhle in Game 4. The game was marked by controversy and again went into extra innings. It was scoreless in the fourth inning and the Phillies had two runners on when Maddox hit a soft liner to the mound. Ruhle fielded it cleanly and threw to first base to complete an apparent double play. Howe then ran to tag second base for an apparent and unlikely triple play. But the Phillies stormed out of the dugout, arguing that Ruhle had trapped the ball. Plate umpire Doug Harvey consulted with fellow umpires and even brought National League president Chub Feeney into the discussion. The argument lasted 20 minutes and the umpires eventually ruled it was a double play because time was called before Howe ran over to tag second base for the third out.

The Astros broke through against Carlton with single runs in the fourth and fifth to take a 2–0 lead. They missed a chance to add another run in the sixth when Gary Woods left third base too soon on a sacrifice fly and was called out after the Phillies appealed the play.

Just six outs away from advancing to the World Series, the Astros could not hold the two-run lead in the eighth inning. Greg Gross and Lonnie Smith started the rally with consecutive singles. After Rose delivered an RBI single off Ruhle, Schmidt followed with a tying RBI single off Dave Smith. Trillo's sacrifice fly gave the Phillies a 3–2 lead, but Warren Brusstar gave up the tying run in the ninth to send the game into extra innings.

The Phillies answered in the tenth with a pair of runs. Rose singled and scored on a double by Luzinski, who was not in the starting lineup for the first time in the series. Trillo followed with another RBI double and McGraw pitched a 1-2-3 inning to nail down a 5–3 win that evened the series at two games apiece.

On paper, Game 5 was a mismatch. Ryan started for the Astros on three days' rest against rookie Marty Bystrom. History was also against the Phillies, as no National League team had ever won a Game 5 on the road.

"I hadn't pitched in 10 days going into that game," Bystrom said. "I remember after Game 4, Dallas came up to me in the clubhouse and said, 'You got the ball tomorrow, kid.' I thought, *Great, I'm ready!* But I was really nervous when I got to the Astrodome the next day. I just told myself to keep the team close until we can get down to the late innings."

With 44,802 fans watching at the Astrodome on a Sunday night, the hometown team opened the scoring on Jose Cruz's RBI double in the first. But the Phillies answered with two runs in the second on Bob Boone's two-run single. The Astros tied it in the sixth with an unearned run after Luzinski's error in left field allowed Walling to reach base. Alan Ashby drove him in with a single.

Bystrom did his job, keeping the Phillies in the game until Christensen relieved him in the bottom of the seventh. Christensen was erratic, however. With two outs and two runners on, Walling singled in the go-ahead run. A wild pitch allowed another run to score and the Astros led 4–2. Ron Reed replaced Christensen and Howe greeted him with an RBI triple to make it 5–2. Once again, the Phillies were six outs away from elimination, and this time they were facing Nolan Ryan.

Larry Bowa was due to lead off the eighth inning, but he had never had much success against Ryan. "Pete Rose came up to me and he said, 'If you get on, we're going to win this damn game.'"

Bowa did his part, hitting Ryan's first pitch to center for a single. Boone came up and also swung at the first pitch. He hit a bouncer to the mound that could have been a double play, but the ball glanced off Ryan's glove, allowing the slow-footed Boone to leg out an infield hit. Greg Gross then put down a perfect bunt and the bases were loaded. Rose walked to force in a run and Ryan was replaced by Joe Sambito. Keith Moreland batted for McBride and drove in a run with a fielder's choice grounder. With runners at first and third and one out, Schmidt stepped to the plate needing only a sacrifice fly to tie the game. Astros manager Bill Virdon called on Game 1 starter Ken Forsch to pitch to Schmidt in the clutch spot. For Schmidt, it was the most important at-bat of his career to that point. All those home-run titles, All-Star appearances, and Gold Gloves meant nothing at that moment. It was up to him to deliver in a crucial situation. Instead, Schmidt struck out looking.

"My big moment, my chance to erase all the doubts back in Philly that I'm a money player. Instead, I strike out, and I got in search of the nearest hole to crawl into," Schmidt said. "In that moment, walking from home to the dugout, I see my entire career flash before me. How can I live down this new failure? No matter what good I did in the past, I've failed in the moment of my team's greatest need. Their offensive leader and highest-paid player, I've blown my greatest opportunity to ever deliver in the clutch."

But pinch-hitter Del Unser bailed Schmidt out with an RBI single to tie the game, and Trillo hit a two-run triple to cap the five-run outburst and give the Phillies a 7–5 lead. Now it was McGraw's turn to hold the lead. But he allowed RBI singles to Rafael Landestoy and Jose Cruz with two outs as the Astros rallied to tie the game.

"I was scared going into that game," McGraw said. "I could tell I was a little off and the hitters were on. The Astrodome was rocking, too. The noise was just phenomenal. It was so loud you could hardly hear yourself think."

The Phillies did not score in the ninth and Dick Ruthven, the Game 2 starter for Philadelphia, pitched a 1-2-3 bottom half to force extra innings for the fourth straight game. Ruthven was upset he did not start the game on three days' rest, but he was told he was being saved to pitch the World Series opener. He grew angrier when he was not the first pitcher out of the bullpen, but he remained focused and did his job with the series on the line.

Schmidt led off the tenth against Frank LaCorte with another strikeout, but Unser followed him with a double. After Trillo flied out, Garry Maddox doubled to knock in Unser. Ruthven came back out to try to get the last three outs and nail down the dramatic win for the Phillies. He quickly got the first two outs before retiring Enos Cabell on a soft liner to Maddox to seal the 8–7 win. The Phillies had won their first pennant in 30 years by beating the Astros in an incredible series that would long be remembered as one of the greatest in baseball history. And they did it with little contribution from Schmidt, who batted .208 in the five games. He was 5-for-24 with one RBI and six strikeouts.

"I remember the joy I felt for our team, coupled with a feeling of acute personal disappointment," Schmidt said. "I guess there was no reason to be that hard on myself, other than that was my nature. Maybe that in itself was a good reason for discomfort in those situations. I didn't relish them the way Pete did. I was simply too afraid to fail, and that affected my ability to succeed under pressure."

Manny Trillo was awarded the NLCS MVP Award after batting .381 with four RBIs. A wild celebration took place inside the visitors' clubhouse at the Astrodome and champagne flowed into the night.

"What's especially nice is that I've never seen a series where so many people contributed to the victory," team owner Ruly Carpenter said while everyone partied in the locker room. "The fact that Garry Maddox got the game winner is most satisfying of all because I know in the back of his mind and the fans' minds was the ball he dropped in the playoffs two years ago in Los Angeles."

The Phillies had desperately needed to advance to the World Series after losing three straight years in the NLCS. They understood it was now or never.

"We had ultimatums given to us all during 1980: 'If you don't win, we're tearing this team apart,'" Bowa said. "It was constantly being written all year. It was like we were on a mission."

Dallas Green had done his job. He ruffled a lot of feathers along the way, but Green pushed all the right buttons and found a way to motivate a group of underachievers to get the most out of their talent.

"The big difference was the manager, as far as demeanor," Bowa said. "Dallas wasn't afraid to step on anyone's toes. He let us know throughout the year that we weren't as good as we thought we were. At the time, we said, 'Who's he?' But looking back on it, he was right. We read too many clippings that we were better than we were."

McGraw pointed to Green's clubhouse tirade in Pittsburgh as the turning point of the season. "As a player I've been in lots of meetings and most of them were bullshit," he said. "This one was real. Dallas called everyone out, challenging our character. It was a slap in the face. What he said went right to the core."

Even Luzinski, who had been at odds with Green throughout the season, had to give the manager credit. "I think Dallas exploded to get us over the hump," he said. "Sometimes you have to take those explosions with a grain of salt. But on that occasion, Dallas forced us to look in the mirror and it produced results."

CHAPTER  7

World Champs!

"Taking the field for the final three outs was surreal. The clock read 11:11, to this day my lucky time. Policemen on horseback ringed the field. I looked at Tug and said, 'Neighbor, let's count 'em down. We need three.'"
—Mike Schmidt

The Philadelphia Phillies were born on May 1, 1883. At first, they were known as the Quakers and entered the National League as a replacement for a team from Worcester, Massachusetts. The Quakers changed their name to the Philadelphias, which was shortened to the Phillies. Both names were used interchangeably until 1890 when Phillies became the official team name. In 1943–44, the Phillies were called the Blue Jays, but that nickname was not popular among fans.

The Quakers played their first game against the Providence Grays before an estimated crowd of 1,200 spectators at Recreation Park on 24th and Columbia avenues in North Philadelphia. The Quakers lost 4–3 to Old Hoss Radbourn and started their season 0–8. They went on to lose 81 of 98 games in their inaugural season.

Losing would become synonymous with the franchise. On July 15, 2007, the Phillies lost their 10,000th game, a 10–2 defeat to the St. Louis Cardinals at Citizens Bank Park in Philadelphia. No team in any professional sport has lost more games than the Phillies. Their existence has been marked by futility, disappointment, and last-place finishes.

The Phillies played 32 seasons before reaching the World Series for the first time in 1915. They lost to the Boston Red Sox in five games after winning the series opener. It took the Phillies 35 more years to reach another World Series. They were swept by the New York Yankees in four games in 1950, losing the first three games by one run.

Ninety-seven seasons had ended without the Phillies winning a championship before they played the Kansas City Royals in the 1980 World Series. They were determined to finally capture that elusive first title.

"The playoffs showed we had become the kind of team that finds a way to win," Mike Schmidt said after that thrilling NLCS series against the Houston Astros. "Of course, we really had so much at stake in that series as well. After our previous playoff losses, we had to get over this hurdle and we did, overcoming everything from the umpiring to the left-on-base records [the Astros and Phillies combined to leave an MLB-record 88 men on base in the five-game series] to win as a team. To be honest, I don't think we could have survived another playoff loss as a team. We were on the edge individually and as a team. The organization would have taken another direction had we lost. But we got over the hurdle. All the negatives of the years before were wiped out by winning the playoffs."

The Royals were among the new kids on the block in the major leagues. They joined the American League as an expansion team in 1969, one year after the Athletics moved from Kansas City to Oakland. Unlike the Phillies, who were terrible for many years, the Royals quickly became one of the most successful franchises in baseball. They had their first winning season in 1971 and won three straight division championships from 1976 through 1978. But just like the Phillies, the Royals failed to win a pennant each time. They lost to the powerhouse Yankees for three consecutive years in the ALCS until breaking through in 1980.

While the Phillies battled the Houston Astros in the NLCS, the Royals faced the Yankees for the AL pennant and had a much easier time. Kansas City swept New York, winning three straight games to advance to the World Series for the first time in the team's brief history. That set up the first World Series since 1920—when the Cleveland Indians beat the Brooklyn Dodgers—in which neither participant had ever won a championship.

Led by rookie manager Jim Frey, the Royals had a talented all-around team with solid hitters and excellent pitchers. All-Star third baseman George Brett was baseball's best hitter in 1980. He batted .390 with 24 homers and 118 RBIs in only 117 games, missing more than a month with injuries. Brett flirted with becoming the first player to bat .400 since Ted Williams hit .406 for the Boston Red Sox in 1941. Brett's average was at .400 on September 19, but a 4-for-27 slump ruined his chances. Still, he had one of the greatest seasons of all time.

First baseman Willie Aikens (.278, 20 HR, 98 RBIs) and designated hitter Hal McRae (.297, 14 HR, 83 RBIs) also provided some pop in Kansas City's lineup, while outfielder Willie Wilson set the table at the top of the order. Wilson batted .326, stole 79 bases, and scored 133 runs. Second baseman Frank White batted .264 during the season, but hit .545 in the ALCS and was named MVP of the series against the Yankees.

Dennis Leonard was the ace of Kansas City's pitching staff; he was 20–11 with a 3.79 ERA. Larry Gura had 18 wins, Paul Splittorff won 14 games, and Rich Gale added 13 victories. Closer Dan Quisenberry led the league with 33 saves in just his second season in the majors.

Before the series started, Mike Schmidt got some advice from Pete Rose, who was seeking his third championship ring in six years. "You're gonna have some fun now," Rose said to Schmidt. "This is the best time of your life. There will be hundreds of writers around. Talk to 'em. Laugh with 'em. Joke with 'em. You relax, enjoy yourself, and pretty soon you'll be playing well."

Game 1 was played before the largest crowd ever at Veterans Stadium. There were 65,791 fans at the Vet on Tuesday, October 14, as the series opened. Manager Dallas Green gave the ball to rookie Bob Walk to pitch the first game because he had used his other starters so much just to get past Houston in the NLCS. The well-rested Royals countered with Leonard, their best pitcher. Walk surrendered two-run homers to Amos Otis and Willie Aikens and the Royals led 4–0 going into the bottom of the third inning.

Leonard retired the first seven batters he faced until Larry Bowa singled with one out in the third. Knowing the Phillies needed a spark, Bowa ignored Green's hold sign and stole second base.

"We were dead. We were just drained. We weren't doing anything," Bowa said. "First pitch, I'm gone. I'm on my own, but Dallas gave me a hold sign because we were four runs down. I thought, *Forget that.* I could get a jump. I had a great jump, but it was a bang-bang play. I mean, boom-boom. I said to myself, 'If I'm out, I might as well keep running.' There was no way I wanted to go back to the dugout to face him. But I was safe."

Bob Boone followed with an RBI double and he later scored on Lonnie Smith's single to left. With two outs, Bake McBride ripped a three-run homer to right field to give the Phillies a 5–4 lead and send the fans into a frenzy. Boone had another RBI double in the fourth and Garry Maddox's sacrifice fly extended the lead to 7–4. Aikens hit another two-run homer, but Tug McGraw pitched two scoreless innings to close out the 7–6 victory. Schmidt had a single in two official at-bats, walked twice, and scored the decisive run. Not a bad start after a disappointing personal effort in the NLCS.

Game 2 was expected to be a pitcher's duel between a pair of lefties, Steve Carlton and Larry Gura. It stayed scoreless until the fifth when the Phillies scored two runs on a sacrifice fly by Trillo and an RBI single by Bowa. But Carlton lost his control in the seventh and the Royals rallied to take a 4–2 lead. Carlton walked the bases loaded before Amos Otis hit a two-run double and John Wathan added a sacrifice fly.

Quisenberry came in early in the seventh to shut the door. The sidearm-throwing right-hander induced three ground outs in the inning. It was a different story in the eighth, however. Boone led off with a walk and scored on a double by pinch-hitter Del Under. McBride's RBI single tied it at 4–4 and brought Schmidt to the plate in a clutch spot. Schmidt jumped on Quisenberry's first pitch and smoked a double to right field. McBride raced home from first to give the Phillies a 5–4 lead. Moreland singled in Schmidt and the Phillies held on for a 6–4 win to take a 2–0 lead in the series.

For the first time in the playoffs, Schmidt was the hero. His big hit off the best reliever in the American League provided the difference. "I did not want to get behind him," Schmidt said. "Quisenberry is a one-pitch pitcher. He's got 33 saves and the best sinker in the American League. I guarantee you he's gonna throw me a good hard first pitch. That was what I was looking for and I got it."

After a day off for travel, the series shifted to Kansas City for Game 3. Dick Ruthven took the mound for the Phillies against Rich Gale. George Brett, who left early the previous game because of a much-publicized case of hemorrhoids, hit a solo homer in the first inning to put the Royals ahead. Schmidt answered with his first career postseason homer, a solo shot that tied the game at 2–2 in the fifth. The score was tied 3–3 after nine innings. In the tenth, Aikens singled in the winning run off McGraw to give Kansas City the victory.

Hoping to even the series, the Royals used Leonard on three days' rest to start Game 4 against Phillies right-hander Larry Christensen. It worked out well for the Royals; Christensen retired just one batter in the first inning and left after giving up four runs. Brett had an RBI triple, Aikens followed with a two-run homer, and Otis added an RBI double. Christensen was yanked for youngster Dickie Noles, who nearly precipitated a bench-clearing brawl by knocking down Brett with a high fastball in the fourth inning.

"Dickie was a gunslinger, the kind of guy you avoided eye contact with in a bar," Schmidt said. "Dickie decided to put an end to this Royals hitting party, so he waited for the right moment. And he got it."

The Royals were leading 5–1 when Noles sent Brett sprawling to the ground. Frey burst out of the dugout and headed for the mound, but Rose stopped the 49-year-old manager before he reached the foul line. Kansas City won the game 5–3 and evened the series at 2–2, but Noles may have given the Royals an uneasy feeling the rest of the series.

"K.C.'s bats calmed down," Schmidt said. "I call it the greatest brushback in World Series history."

For the pivotal Game 5, Green decided to use 22-year-old rookie Marty Bystrom instead of Walk, who allowed six runs in seven innings in the opener. Schmidt launched a homer to deep center field off Larry Gura to give the Phillies a 2–0 lead in the fourth. Bystrom could not keep the Royals' bats quiet for long. Otis led off the bottom of the sixth with a game-tying solo homer and U.L. Washington drove in the go-ahead run with a sacrifice fly after a pair of singles by Clint Hurdle and Darrell Porter started the rally. The score remained 3–2 going into the ninth with Quisenberry on the mound trying to finish it off and put the Phillies on the verge of elimination.

Schmidt led off the inning. Brett moved in a few steps at third base because Schmidt had shown a willingness to try a drag bunt earlier in the series. Perhaps the couple extra steps helped Schmidt because he lined a hard shot that bounced off Brett's glove for a single. "I had no intention of bunting in that situation," Schmidt said. "As a lead-off batter, I was just trying to drive the ball someplace. I did notice that Brett was playing me in, though. And maybe that helped me get on base. If he was playing me even with or just behind the bag he might have had the time to make the play."

Del Unser came up next as a pinch-hitter for Lonnie Smith. He smoked a double to right field and Schmidt sprinted all the way from first to score the tying run. Quisenberry got the next two outs before Manny Trillo delivered a run-scoring single to put Philadelphia ahead 4–3. McGraw made everyone sweat it out in the ninth. He walked the bases loaded before striking out Jose Cardenal to end the game. The Phillies took a 3–2 lead in the series and returned to Philadelphia needing one more win to become world champions.

The stage was set for the Phillies. They had their ace on the mound, the man they called "Lefty." They had 65,838 screaming fans behind them. All they had to do was win one more game to exorcise the demons from the past 97 seasons and be rid of the nightmares of the collapse of 1964 that still haunted the city and the franchise. Game 6 against the Royals was played on Tuesday, October 21.

The City of Philadelphia, which owned Veterans Stadium, wanted to ensure that fans would not cause destruction during a potential victory celebration. So, Wilson Goode, the city's managing director, ordered extra security. He brought in mounted police and riot control officers with K-9 dogs to surround the stadium. Phillies vice president Bill Giles was concerned the dogs might be another black eye for a city that already had a reputation for boorish behavior. But Goode insisted it was the only way to ensure safety. The stadium's grounds crew and security staff and the city's police department were all in place by the morning of the game.

Schmidt rode to the stadium that afternoon with his neighbor, Tug McGraw. Driving to the ballpark together became a superstition for the All-Star third baseman and the veteran closer that season. They would stop and get the same black-and-white milkshakes and followed the exact routine every day. On their way to Game 6, Schmidt and McGraw planned their victory celebration.

"He predicted that he'd drive in the winning run and make some great defensive play and that I'd come in, pitch the last inning, and get the big strikeout to end it," McGraw recalled. "'When that happens,' he said, 'I'm going to run over and dive on top of you so I can get my picture on the front page of the newspaper, maybe on the cover of *Sports Illustrated.*'"

Phillies shortstop Larry Bowa was confident, too. He had a strong feeling the Phillies were going to win it that night. "I never, ever would say anything is a lock, but when I went out that door that day I told my wife, Sheena, that we were going to win," he said. "Carlton was going. The crowd had been waiting for hundreds of years. The day before you could feel it. You go to the store. You go driving around. People would be waving at you. I had never had a feeling like that in my life. This is over."

Rich Gale started for the Royals on three days' rest. He allowed only two runs in Game 3, but was yanked in the fifth inning of that game after giving up seven hits and three walks. The Phillies wanted to get to him early, give Carlton a cushion, and build on it.

Carlton fanned two batters in the first inning and escaped trouble by inducing a double-play grounder in the second. The Phillies got on the board first in the third inning. Bob Boone walked, Lonnie Smith reached on second baseman Frank White's error, and Pete Rose's bunt single loaded the bases for Schmidt, who had popped out his first time up. Gale threw a fastball on the inside part of the plate and Schmidt lined it to right field to score Boone and Smith for a 2–0 lead. When he reached first base, Schmidt was so excited about the hit that he pumped his fist, a rare display of emotion from Mr. Cool. "I couldn't have gotten a bigger hit than that," he said.

Carlton was brilliant with the lead and the Phillies tacked on single runs in the fifth and sixth to make it 4–0. Lefty entered the eighth working on a three-hitter, but left after a walk and a single to the first two batters. Dallas Green called on Tug McGraw to make his fourth appearance of the series and to pitch out of another jam. The Tugger got out of the inning with a 4–1 lead. Dan Quisenberry, who pitched in every game of the series, retired the Phillies in order in the bottom of the eighth and McGraw took the mound needing to get three more outs.

"Taking the field for the final three outs was surreal," Schmidt said. "The clock read 11:11, to this day my lucky time. Policemen on horseback ringed the field. I looked at Tug and said, 'Neighbor, let's count 'em down. We need three.'"

McGraw, the eccentric left-hander, had pitched in these situations before. He led the New York Mets to the NL pennant in 1973, coining the phrase "Ya gotta believe!" along the way. McGraw had an off year in 1979, posting a 5.14 ERA despite getting 16 saves. They called him "Grand Slam McGraw" because he gave up four slams in one season. General manager Paul Owens and manager Dallas Green thought the 35-year-old reliever was finished, so they put him on the trading block that winter. A deal that would have sent McGraw and right fielder Bake McBride to the Texas Rangers for former AL Cy Young Award winner Sparky Lyle was nixed by team owner Ruly Carpenter. (Philadelphia acquired Lyle in a separate deal in September of 1980.) McGraw rewarded Carpenter's faith by saving 20 games and recording the lowest ERA of his career (1.46). He missed a month of the season because of arm injuries, but pitched through the pain and provided the Phillies with the emotional leadership they needed. McGraw was the spirit of the team. He wore his heart on his sleeve, made everyone laugh, and kept the mood light. McGraw never made things easy, however. And the ninth inning of Game 6 would be no different.

After striking out Amos Otis to start the inning, McGraw issued a walk and two singles to load the bases. With the tying run on first base, McGraw got Frank White to hit a foul pop near the Phillies' dugout. Catcher Bob Boone leapt from behind the plate and called for the ball as he and first baseman Pete Rose converged. The ball popped out of Boone's mitt, but Rose was there to squeeze it for the second out.

"It wasn't my ball," Boone said. "I got to the end of the dugout and I'm listening for Pete to call me off, but I don't hear him. I can see the ball coming down, plus I'm real close to the edge of the dugout. I'm still listening for Pete and I don't hear anything. 'Where is he?' I'm asking myself, 'Where the hell is he?' As the ball is getting closer and closer I'm thinking, *I know he's going to crash into me but I just can't let the ball drop because he's not saying anything.*

Despite struggling through his first full year in the majors in 1973, Mike Schmidt quickly established himself as one of the most feared sluggers in the National League.

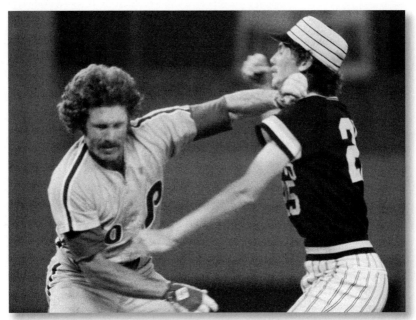

Believed by many to be too stoic and lackadaisical, Schmidt fractured that perception—and his finger—when he fought with Pittsburgh Pirates pitcher Bruce Kison in 1977.

Schmidt led the Phillies to three straight National League East titles from 1976 to 1978, a period during which he hit 97 home runs.

Schmidt, Larry Bowa, Manny Trillo, and Pete Rose formed the Phillies infield during their 1980 championship season.

Schmidt and the Phillies celebrated the first title in franchise history after beating the Kansas City Royals in Game 6 of the 1980 World Series.

Schmidt showed his playful side in 1985, donning a wig and sunglasses before heading onto the field for a home game against the Chicago Cubs.

Schmidt remained focused on his family throughout his storied career, even playing catch with his son Jonathan prior to the 1987 All-Star Game in Oakland, California.

Phillies fans cheered as Schmidt collected his third NL MVP Award in 1986; he remains one of only 10 players in MLB history to accomplish that feat.

Fighting back tears, Schmidt announced his retirement from the game in 1989.

Phillies legends Richie Ashburn and Mike Schmidt were inducted into the National Baseball Hall of Fame in 1995. Schmidt received an astounding 96.5 percent of the vote.

In 2004, Schmidt and the Phillies unveiled a statue honoring the third baseman's career near the third-base gate outside Citizens Bank Park in Philadelphia.

Though he has never been given the opportunity to be a big-league manager, Schmidt has shared his wisdom with current Phillies, including first baseman Ryan Howard, as an occasional hitting instructor.

"Normally I'd let the ball fall to me, but I figured I was going to have to outrebound Pete for this ball, so I went up to grab it. It was like trying to catch a ball with a wooden board, the ball just sprang up on me. When the ball popped out of the glove, I remember thinking, *Oh my god! I've never dropped one of these in my life!* But I dropped it because I was trying to catch it differently to avoid getting hit. At first, I was mad at Pete. I wanted to kill him. It was his ball. Then, all of a sudden, this glove appears and he catches the ball, so then I wanted to kiss him!"

The crowd was going absolutely berserk at that point in anticipation of the final out. Policemen on their horses and riot officers holding attack dogs took their positions along the first- and third-base sides in foul territory. Willie Wilson stepped to the plate. Wilson had an outstanding season as the Royals' leadoff hitter, but he already had struck out 11 times, setting a World Series record. Boone walked out to the mound, partly to discuss strategy but mainly to relax after a mentally exhausting play. He implored McGraw to throw one more screwball, his signature pitch, to set Wilson up for a fastball. McGraw had little left in his arm and his fingers were numb.

First pitch: screwball for a strike. Second pitch: slider for strike two. Everyone in the stands was standing and the stadium was rocking. McGraw threw a high fastball that missed the plate. Wilson was perfectly set up for a 1–2 screwball, but McGraw reached back and uncorked a fastball on the inside part of the plate. Wilson swung and missed. Game over. The Philadelphia Phillies were World Series champions for the first time in the franchise's history.

McGraw leaped off the mound, arms raised high over his head. The dugout emptied and players and coaches stormed the field. McGraw turned toward Schmidt, who was racing in from third base just as they had planned hours earlier. Schmidt dove into McGraw's arms atop a pile of players and the celebration was on. It was a rare display of emotion by Schmidt, and photographers captured the picture for posterity.

Fans stayed in the stands because the police and their snarling dogs made sure no one jumped onto the field. They watched the players celebrate and partied on their own. In the streets of South Philadelphia, people ran outside their homes, banging pots and pans. Drivers honked their horns and others danced in the streets from Broad Street to North Philly and into the suburbs.

Schmidt was named MVP of the World Series after batting .381 with two homers and seven RBIs. He came through when the team needed him most, erasing all the doubts created by years of playoff failures and frustrations.

"I thought he was a little bit nervous at first," teammate Del Unser said. "But then he came on and kept stroking the ball. Then he was beautiful. He gets the big hit tonight. He did it when we needed it. He's just been super."

Schmidt downplayed his contributions and credited other players, especially Bowa. "Larry Bowa had an outstanding World Series," he said. "He could easily have been named the MVP. I guess they chose me because I had a little more notoriety during the regular season. Although I had seven RBIs in the Series, Larry had [one] more hit than the eight I collected. He was also exceptional in the field. I'd have been just as happy if he had won the award."

In the stands, Schmidt was the people's choice. The fans held a large sign during Game 6 that read "Mike Schmidt For President." The same fans who booed Schmidt during his slumps and made his life miserable at various points in his career now viewed him as a hero.

When Schmidt first entered the clubhouse five minutes after the game ended, he appeared to be in disbelief. He had a blank look on his face and was not even smiling as people congratulated him. "I'm still sort of in a coma," he said.

Schmidt finally smiled when Dallas Green raised the championship trophy in the air and yelled, "Look at this! Look at this, Schmitty!"

It was the culmination of a lifelong dream. The young kid from Dayton, Ohio, who overcame bad knees and long odds to make the majors had become a world champion and an MVP. But Schmidt's excitement was tempered somewhat during the celebration as he reflected on his grandmother's death in September.

"She was the first person to throw a baseball to me," Schmidt said. "That was the only prayer of mine that wasn't answered down the stretch."

Schmidt talked about his faith in God and the image of the Phillies as an unlikable team that could not win the big game. "I play this game to glorify God, to tell you the truth," he said.

As for the team's image, the only thing that mattered was that they had finally won. "People are looking at the world champions," Schmidt said. "The magazine writers are going to come to Clearwater first next spring. People will be watching us and what we do. That's a good feeling."

A day later, the city celebrated the Phillies and their World Series victory with a ticker-tape parade down Broad Street. Players, coaches, and front office personnel rode in a motorcade as more than 1 million people lined the streets and partied. The parade route ended at John F. Kennedy Stadium in South Philly, where 85,000 fans jammed into the seats and cheered while players took turns on the microphone addressing the crowd. McGraw whipped them into a frenzy when he grabbed a copy of the *Philadelphia Daily News* with its "We Win" headline, thrust it in the air over his head, and shouted, "All throughout baseball history, Philadelphia has taken a back seat to New York City. Well, New York City can take this world championship and stick it 'cause we're No. 1!"

Schmidt was far more humble. He was overwhelmed by the outpouring of support from the fans and their affection for the Phillies. It seemed like all the negativity in the past had disappeared and a new, loving relationship was created.

"I never saw so many sincere faces in my life as I did in that parade today," he said. "Take this world championship and savor it. You all deserve it."

Two weeks later, the Baseball Writers Association of America unanimously chose Mike Schmidt as the National League's Most Valuable Player for the 1980 season. He became just the second player in the history of the award to sweep all the ballots. Schmidt thanked God, his grandmother, and Pete Rose.

"Pete instilled in me a new vitality for playing the game at this point in my career," Schmidt said. "Being 31 years old, which is a turning point for a lot of ballplayers, he gave me a great outlook on the game of baseball, a feeling of youth, and a feeling of wanting to have fun on the baseball field. Pete came along at a great time in my career and I'm thankful for that."

The honors and awards kept rolling in for Schmidt. The city of Philadelphia honored him as Grand Marshal of its 1980 Thanksgiving Day parade. The Philadelphia Sportswriters Association named him professional athlete of the year. It was at that banquet in January 1981 when Schmidt uttered his famous quote: "Only in Philadelphia can you experience the thrill of victory one night, and the agony of reading about it the next day."

At least his MVP performance and the team's World Series victory ensured it would be all positives until spring training came around and a new season was underway.

CHAPTER

Cashing In

"So much for our dynasty."

—Mike Schmidt

Winning a championship and being named Most Valuable Player of both the regular season and the World Series had a significant impact on Mike Schmidt's life and the way others viewed him. People stopped criticizing his mental approach to the game and his nonchalant attitude, and no one questioned his ability to hit in clutch situations anymore.

Now Schmidt was the player teammates turned to for advice on hitting. His constant tinkering at the plate paid off when he found the perfect stance that worked for him. "I went to that off-the-plate, deep-in-the-box stance because I was having trouble with the pitches on the inside part of the plate," he said. "Now I can hit that pitch consistently and I feel very comfortable. All the good hitters I've ever seen stride into the ball or into the plate. George Brett hits that way. Roberto Clemente hit that way."

Schmidt was still considered a streaky hitter who was prone to slumps, but he had a better handle on figuring things out. "I'm never going to say, 'Hey, I know how to stop a slump,' or 'I know how to prevent going 0-for-15,'" he said. "But I feel I have a pretty good grip on my batting style, and a pretty good knowledge of how things go wrong when they go wrong, and a pretty good knowledge of why things are right when they go right."

Schmidt was at the top of his game when he arrived in Clearwater for spring training in 1981. The reigning NL MVP was hoping to lead his team to consecutive World Series titles; there was local talk that the Phillies had the makings of a dynasty. But many national baseball writers had their doubts about the Phillies. *Sports Illustrated* picked the Montreal Expos to win the NL East, saying the Phillies were "headed for a breakdown." The team that showed up for the start of spring training was the same one that won the championship several months earlier. Before camp broke, however, general manager Paul Owens and manager Dallas Green shook things up with a couple of trades.

First, the Phillies traded left-hander Randy Lerch to Milwaukee for reserve outfielder Dick Davis on March 1. Lerch lost his spot in the starting rotation in 1980 by going 4–14 and had been left off the postseason roster.

A few weeks later, right-handed pitcher Bob Walk was sent to Atlanta for outfielder Gary Matthews. Walk won 11 games as a rookie and got the victory in Game 1 of the World Series, but the 30-year-old Matthews was only one year removed from an All-Star season. To make room for Matthews in the outfield, the Phillies sold Greg Luzinski to the Chicago White Sox just one week before the regular season started.

Luzinski was a popular player in Philadelphia and had spent his entire career with the Phillies after being drafted in the first round of the 1968 amateur draft. But he struggled in 1980 (batting a career-worst .228), spent time in Green's doghouse, and was benched for three games in the World Series even though managers were able to use a designated hitter for each game.

"That was a sad day for Phillies fans, who would see most of the team depart over the next couple of years," Schmidt said. "So much for our dynasty."

The season began under the threat of another players' strike. The labor contract had expired on December 31, 1979, and the entire 1980 season was played without a new deal. Contract negotiations broke down before spring training opened and team owners made sure they were prepared for a strike by purchasing insurance from Lloyds of London. That put the players at a great disadvantage. Nonetheless, the season opened for the Phillies at Cincinnati on April 8.

Schmidt was 0-for-2 with two walks in a 3–2 loss to the Reds before embarking on a 13-game hitting streak. The Phillies resumed their winning ways and Schmidt continued hitting. He had five home runs and 14 RBIs in April and the Phillies went 12–6. Though he had shown another side by displaying his emotions after the final out of the World Series, Schmidt was his same old cool self. There was no reason for him to mess with an approach that worked for him.

"I want to convey to my teammates and to the opposition that I'm in control of myself," Schmidt explained. "I don't want anyone to think I am intimidated by anything that goes on out on the field, whether it's being done well or poorly. I always like to keep the opposition feeling I'm in control of myself, especially offensively. I feel that in order to succeed as a hitter, you have to have as much poise as you can possibly have while you're hitting. The same is true defensively. The more tension and pressure you put on yourself as a fielder, the more balls are apt to carom off your body and go too far away for you to field them. But if the ball takes a bad hop and hits a loose, relaxed, limp body, it's more apt to just drop straight down. Sometimes, maybe I appear too cool on the outside. But there are times when I'm battling negative thoughts."

The Phillies were two games ahead of St. Louis for first place when the season came to a screeching halt on June 10. The players went out on strike, making it the fifth work stoppage in Major League Baseball history. Owners wanted more control over players and demanded compensation for losing a player through free agency; players maintained that any form of compensation would undermine the value of becoming a free agent. Negotiations between the two sides were bitter and the strike lasted for seven weeks.

Schmidt was hitting .284 with 14 homers and 41 RBIs when the players walked out. He took advantage of the unplanned vacation by spending more time at home with his wife, daughter, and new son, Jonathan. Schmidt also began preparing for a future after baseball by taking a job with WCAU-TV in Philadelphia as a sports commentator on its Sunday night telecasts. In his first editorial, Schmidt stirred some controversy by criticizing the owners for the strike and defending the players, saying they "earnestly tried to settle the dispute, voting to go on strike as a last resort."

Critics questioned Schmidt's ability to offer objective commentary on the subject when he was a high-salaried player who stood to lose a lot of money, but he defended his view. "I'm not a baseball player when I'm doing the news. I'm a newscaster," he said. "I really felt I wanted to give the public some meat in my debut. The strike is a hot issue. I didn't say anything that wasn't an exact fact. If an owner wants to come on as a guest or something to state facts, he's welcome."

The strike finally ended on July 31 after 50 days of the season had been lost. Players lost an estimated $146 million in salaries while owners lost an estimated $72 million in revenues. Play resumed with the All-Star Game on August 9 at Cleveland Stadium in Cleveland, Ohio. Schmidt made his sixth appearance in the Midsummer Classic and hit a two-run homer off reliever Rollie Fingers in the eighth inning to lift the National League to a 5–4 victory.

Because the strike canceled so many games, the season was split into two halves. Teams who were first in their division at the time of the strike automatically clinched a postseason berth. The Phillies led the NL East, so they were guaranteed a playoff spot no matter their record after the strike. Perhaps that was a major reason they were so lackluster to start the second half, losing seven of their first nine games.

While the team struggled, Schmidt was on another level. He hit at a torrid pace in August and was named Player of the Month after batting .380 with nine homers and 24 RBIs in 20 games. Schmidt stayed hot in September and finished the season with a .316 average, 31 homers, and 91 RBIs in only 102 games. He won his fifth home-run title and was named NL MVP for the second consecutive year, becoming the ninth player in major league history to win the award two straight seasons.

"Maybe I benefited from the time off I had with my family," Schmidt said. "Maybe it was the fact that we'd won the first half. It seemed that every at-bat was not a do-or-die situation."

Despite his success that season, Schmidt was not immune to criticism from manager Dallas Green. Tired of the team's lackadaisical approach, Green fired a few verbal shots at Schmidt. "I don't think he's as prepared as he thinks he is for playing the game," Green said, referring to Schmidt's preference for skipping infield practice. "There's a pattern there, the throwing error in the early innings of a ballgame. It would be better for the team if he took infield practice. If, in fact, he's a true leader, he's got to be out there. Okay, maybe it's surface stuff, but it ties in with being a super-class guy."

The Phillies finished 25–27 in the second half and were not considered favorites to repeat as World Series champions when they entered the postseason. The Montreal Expos finished first in the NL East in the second half, setting up a best-of-five first-round playoff series.

The Expos won the first two games in Montreal, but the Phillies evened the series with two wins at home. In Game 5 at Veterans Stadium, Expos ace Steve Rogers tossed a six-hit shutout and Montreal advanced to the NLCS with a 3–0 victory. Schmidt was 4-for-16 with one homer in the series.

After the season, the organization underwent major changes. Dallas Green stepped down as manager and left Philadelphia to become the general manager of the Chicago Cubs. Owner Ruly Carpenter, frustrated by the demands of running a baseball team in the new era of free agency, sold the Phillies, ending almost four decades of ownership by his family. Bill Giles, the executive vice president of the Phillies, headed an investment group that purchased the team from Carpenter. Giles hired Pat Corrales to replace Green and immediately began working on a new long-term contract for Schmidt, who was set to become a free agent.

Schmidt had established himself as the top third baseman at a time when several stars played that position. Ron Cey, Bill Madlock, and Bob Horner in the National League and George Brett, Graig Nettles, and Buddy Bell in the American League were the cream of the crop. Schmidt was widely considered to be the best of the All-Star bunch. Now, as a free agent, he was set to cash in on his success.

With the advent of free agency, salaries escalated across the sport. Reggie Jackson got a megadeal from the New Yankees worth $2.3 million over five years. The Boston Red Sox gave Jim Rice a seven-year contract worth $770,000 annually. Dave Parker signed a five-year contract with the Pittsburgh Pirates for $900,000 per season. Nolan Ryan of the Houston Astros was the first player to average $1 million per year on his contract.

A few days before Christmas, the Phillies and Schmidt agreed on a six-year contract worth $10 million. It made him the highest-paid player in National League history and second only to Dave Winfield, who got a 10-year, $23 million contract from the New York Yankees.

"He's the best player in the big leagues," general manager Paul Owens said of Schmidt.

Giles called Schmidt a "special commodity." "Our philosophy is that you have to take care of four or five key guys like Rose, Schmidt, Steve Carlton, Gary Matthews," he said. "You have to treat everybody fairly, but we can't afford to lose one of those four guys. You always worry about morale. It goes through your mind. But I think you have to take a look at what you think is the best thing for the bottom line. You can't worry about petty jealousy and squabbles."

Schmidt knew he would be referred to now as a "Ten Million Dollar Man," and he had to live up to even higher expectations from fans and the media. The new contract meant that Schmidt probably could finish his career in Philadelphia. He finally felt at peace in the city and had earned respect from the demanding fans. Philadelphia was his wife's hometown and he wanted his children to have a stable home life.

"Fans are going to say, 'Let's see how he plays now, let's see if he tails off now,'" Schmidt said. "While I can't guarantee good years simply because you can't guarantee anything in baseball, I can handle that sort of pressure. I can tell you one thing: I'm going to be playing as hard as I've ever played and doing my best to improve. I'm not going to be satisfied with the level of the game I'm playing now. I'm going to try to get better, not because I make more money, but just because I have that kind of respect for the game."

* * *

The dismantling of the 1980 team continued after the '81 season. Lonnie Smith was traded to the St. Louis Cardinals in November, Bob Boone was sold to the California Angels in December, and Keith Moreland and Dickie Noles went to Dallas Green's Cubs two days after that deal. That was just the start.

In late January, Green pulled off one of the most lopsided trades in sports history. He sent shortstop Ivan DeJesus to Philadelphia for Larry Bowa and a throw-in named Ryne Sandberg, who appeared in 13 games with the Phillies the previous September. DeJesus hit .249 in three seasons with the Phillies. Sandberg, meanwhile, was a 10-time All-Star during 15 seasons with the Cubs, won the 1984 NL MVP Award, and was voted into the Hall of Fame in 2005. Bowa said he helped orchestrate the deal.

"So they finally put the deal together. The Chicago writers call me up," Bowa said. "And I didn't know the final trade yet. So I asked, 'Who's the guy they threw in?' When they said Sandberg, I told them, 'Well then I was the guy they threw in because Sandberg is going to be a great player.' And the guy says, 'Come on.' I said, 'I'm telling you. He's going to be an unbelievable player.' Of course, I was proven right on that one."

Completing the Phillies' overhaul, Bake McBride was traded to the Indians in February. So the Phillies entered spring training with only four starting position players—Mike Schmidt, Pete Rose, Manny Trillo, and Garry Maddox—remaining from the team that won the World Series just two years earlier. Gone were Boone, Bowa, Luzinski, McBride, Smith, and Moreland, among others.

Schmidt now was surrounded by a new group of teammates, but his goal was clear. He wanted to become the first player ever to win three straight MVP Awards. But those hopes were dashed quickly when he tore his rib cage muscle in the fifth game of the season. Schmidt missed the next 14 games before returning to the lineup on May 1. It would take several weeks before Schmidt could play without pain. The injury affected his power more than his overall batting. Schmidt hit three homers in his first week back from the disabled list, but then he went nearly a month without hitting another one. After connecting off San Francisco's John Montefusco on May 8, Schmidt did not go deep in his next 87 at-bats until finally hitting a homer off Chicago's Dickie Noles on June 7. Schmidt batted .345 (30-for-87) in that span, prompting Corrales to joke about moving him into the leadoff spot in the lineup.

"Mike is a perfectionist," Corrales said. "He wants to hit 40 homers, 120 RBIs, and finish with a .300 average. That's the perfect baseball player. Now there's nothing wrong with that kind of thing, but it does take its toll on a player, even of his caliber."

Losing Schmidt for most of April hurt the Phillies, and they were still trying to catch up in the division standings after he returned. A five-game losing streak dropped Philadelphia 5½ games behind the Cardinals by mid-June. But the Phillies went on an 11–3 run and moved into a tie for first after Steve Carlton beat the Cardinals 1–0 on June 28. The teams went back and forth over the next three months. Schmidt found his power stroke after the All-Star break, hitting 14 homers in a 24-game span from July 17 to August 10.

The Cardinals had a half-game lead over the Phillies when they visited Veterans Stadium for a critical three-game series that began on September 13. Carlton tossed a three-hitter and hit a solo homer in a 2–0 win that pushed the Phillies ahead of St. Louis. The next night, the Phillies trailed 2–0 when Schmidt came to the plate against Bruce Sutter with the bases loaded and one out in the bottom of the eighth inning. Schmidt hit a grounder back to the mound that started a home-to-first double play to end the rally. The Cardinals won that game and the next one to take a 1½-game lead over the Phillies. Schmidt fell into a slump at the worst possible time. He went 0-for-20 as the Phillies lost five of six games to drop to 5½ games out of first place over the next week. They never recovered, finishing in second place behind the Cardinals.

Critics pointed the finger at Schmidt for failing to deliver in the heat of the pennant race, but Corrales and Rose were quick to defend the superstar. "You can't blame just one man," Corrales said. "You can't blame just Mike Schmidt."

Rose felt other players around Schmidt had not done enough to pick up the slack. Gary Matthews and Bo Diaz also slumped at the same time. "I don't think it's fair to put the load on his shoulders," Rose said. "When we've got guys not swinging the bat, he feels he has to get three hits and hit two out of the ballpark and that puts too much strain on him. He's the best player in the league, but if we don't set the table, he can't knock in runs. It's been a team effort. Everybody from top to bottom had chances to knock in runs. Schmitty's hot streak got us back in this thing. With any good team, if one or two guys slump, one or two other guys have got to get hot and pick up the pieces."

Schmidt finished the season with a .280 average, 35 homers, and 87 RBIs. He fell short of his goal of winning three straight MVP Awards, placing sixth in the voting. Dale Murphy, who led the Atlanta Braves to the NL West division title, earned MVP honors. Overall, Schmidt had done well to overcome a tough injury that hampered him for a couple of months. Still, he was disappointed with the season.

"If you base my performance on statistics, I've played the game in previous years at a level that is hard to match," he said. "When you set those kinds of standards for yourself, you also set them for the people who watch you. In that sense, I guess I was in a slump this year. But I look at what I achieved, the things I accomplished in only three good months, and I can't help wondering what kind of numbers I could have produced if I had six good months."

CHAPTER

9

The Wheeze Kids

"I was constantly trying to adjust and it almost seemed like they knew what I was thinking. I tried as hard as I could, but it just didn't work out. I apologize for my performance, but not for my effort."
—Mike Schmidt

Years after helping the Cincinnati Reds win two World Series titles, Pete Rose, Joe Morgan, and Tony Perez were reunited on the Philadelphia Phillies. The former members of the Big Red Machine were aging players on the downside of their careers, but they had enough left in their old tanks to help the Phillies make a run at another World Series.

The Phillies already had a veteran squad before Perez (40) and Morgan (39) arrived in 1983. Rose was 41, reliever Ron Reed was 40, ace Steve Carlton and closer Tug McGraw were 38, and Mike Schmidt was 33. In all, 22 of the players on the 40-man roster in spring training were at least 30 years old. People started poking fun at the Phillies because they had so many older players. Everyone wanted to give them a nickname, and since the 1950 Phillies were called the Whiz Kids because of their youthfulness, this group was dubbed the Wheeze Kids.

General manager Paul Owens started reshaping the roster by trading second baseman Manny Trillo to Cleveland in the heavily criticized five-for-one deal that brought heralded prospect Von Hayes to Philadelphia. With Trillo gone, the Phillies needed a second baseman to fill the gap until youngster Juan Samuel was ready. So Owens dealt pitcher Mike Krukow to San Francisco for Morgan and closer Al Holland. Owens then signed Perez to provide depth on the bench and give Rose an occasional day off at first base.

Rose, Perez, and Morgan had not played together since helping the Reds capture their second straight World Series championship in 1976. Once they got together in spring training with the Phillies, it was just like old times.

"They kept replaying the '75 World Series during infield drills," Schmidt said after practice one day. "Perez said they wouldn't be wearing world champion rings if he hadn't hit Bill Lee's let-up pitch out of the park. Morgan said they wouldn't have rings if he hadn't had two game-winning hits, and Rose said he hit .370 in the series."

That type of repartee was common among the trio all spring. They pushed each other and enjoyed being on the same field again. "I know

Pete as well as I know anybody," Morgan said. "I know when to kick him in the rear, and I know when to pat him on the back. People don't think he needs that stuff anymore, but he does."

Rose was coming off a season in which he batted just .271, the second-lowest average of his career. He had not missed a game in four seasons with the Phillies, and manager Pat Corrales figured giving Rose a day off sometimes would help him in the long run. Of course, Rose hated the idea. "I'll rest plenty when I'm dead," he said.

Schmidt loved having the former Big Red Machine stars in Phillies pinstripes. He even played along when they went back and forth at each other. One day during a morning practice, Schmidt rolled up his sleeves and pretended to be former Reds slugger and coach Ted Kluszewski.

"Imagine, sharing a clubhouse with three of the greatest Reds of all time," Schmidt said. "Those guys were amazing to be around. They talked trash all day, every day, and had forgotten more about winning than most teams ever knew."

Rose, who had not played in the outfield in five years, moved to right field to make room for Perez in the lineup and all three players started on Opening Day. Rose led off, Morgan batted second, and Perez hit fifth behind Schmidt. The Phillies dropped their first three games, but then won five in a row and nine of 10. Schmidt started slow, going 3-for-22 before he came around. In late May, Schmidt slumped again and so did the Phillies. They had lost six straight games going into the middle game of a three-game series at home against the Montreal Expos on May 28. Schmidt entered the contest hitless in his last 18 at-bats and things got uglier once the game started. He struck out in each of his first four at-bats, doing so on just 12 pitches. The fans, mostly frustrated by the team's recent performance, took it out on Schmidt. They booed him when he headed back to the dugout after he went down swinging in the fifth and took a called third strike in the seventh.

"If I swung, I missed. If I took, it was a strike," Schmidt said. "I challenge anyone to strike out four times on 12 pitches."

Rain delayed the game and Schmidt sought comfort in the locker room. Perez lifted his spirits during a brief chat. When the game resumed, Schmidt got another chance to redeem himself in the ninth. The score was tied at 3–3 and the winning run was on second base when Schmidt stepped up against Expos closer Jeff Reardon. He slammed a two-run homer to win the game, snapping a 0-for-22 skid and giving the Phillies a much-needed victory. It was Schmidt's first homer in 16 games.

"That's it," he said afterward. "I'm not talking about my 0-fers anymore."

Despite hitting the game-winning shot, Schmidt continued to struggle at the plate. His average dropped into the .250s and .240s while the Phillies kept playing up-and-down ball. Fortunately for them, the NL East was a weak division that season and none of the teams could build a big lead in the standings.

Owens was unhappy with the team's mediocre performance, so he fired Corrales after a loss to Cincinnati on July 17. The Phillies were 43–42 at the time and tied for first with St. Louis. Corrales became the first manager to ever be fired while his team led the division. Owens was convinced by others in the front office to go down to the dugout and manage the team himself. This was not a totally new assignment for Owens, who managed the Phillies for 80 games during the 1972 season. But the players had a tough time adjusting to the new man in charge and the different lineups he kept posting.

Schmidt had a difficult summer. He took a lot of criticism from the media and even considered boycotting the press like teammate Steve Carlton. In early September, Schmidt took out his frustrations on management instead.

"We have no sense of direction. We have developed no stability," Schmidt ranted to reporters. "Nobody is sure who the manager is. We're the least likely of the four teams to get hot in September because we don't have any kind of foundation for the guys to build on. How can a guy get scalding hot with the bat if he's not going to play every day? As a veteran player on the Philadelphia Phillies, I'm disappointed in the way the front office has handled this year. We got a team full of guys that are capable of turning on a switch, and you wouldn't know it's the same ballclub two weeks later. But we've got an organization full of soap opera problems that are cutting into the chances of that happening."

Owens did not appreciate Schmidt's uncharacteristic tongue-lashing and responded quickly. "Schmidt's problem is that he thinks too much. He should just go out and play the game, using the ability God gave him," he said.

Schmidt's comments may have ruffled some feathers, but his teammates were glad to know their leader had their backs. Soon after the smoke cleared, the Phillies went on a big run. They won 11 straight games to take a 4½-game lead over the Pittsburgh Pirates in the division with five games remaining. A day after the winning streak ended, the Phillies clinched their fifth division championship in eight years with a 13–6 win over the Cubs at Wrigley Field. Schmidt hit his league-leading 40th homer in the victory and sat out the final three games against the Pirates. He finished the season with a .255 average and 109 RBIs to go with his sixth career home-run title.

On paper, the 1983 National League Championship Series was an overwhelming mismatch. The NL West champion Los Angeles Dodgers dominated the Phillies during the regular season, winning 11 out of 12 games. Five of the wins were shutouts. The Phillies entered the series looking not only to redeem themselves for their futile effort against Los Angeles that year, but to avenge losses in the NLCS in 1977 and 1978.

Game 1 at Dodger Stadium was a pitching duel between two left-handers. Steve Carlton, who earned his 300th career win in September, went head-to-head against Jerry Reuss. Schmidt clubbed a solo homer to dead center in the first inning and Carlton made sure that was enough. Lefty scattered seven hits over 7⅔ innings and Al Holland got the last four outs to preserve the 1–0 victory. Holland, who was nicknamed "Mr. T," escaped a bases-loaded jam in the eighth by retiring Mike Marshall on a fly ball to right.

The Dodgers evened the series with a 4–1 win behind Fernando Valenzuela in Game 2. Valenzuela outdueled John Denny, who was the NL Cy Young Award winner in his first full season with the Phillies. Denny got little help from his defense; errors by shortstop Ivan DeJesus and center fielder Garry Maddox allowed three unearned runs to score.

The series moved to Veterans Stadium for Game 3. The Phillies knew they needed to get more offense after scoring just two runs in the first two games. Gary Matthews, who had a terrible regular season, provided the hitting. Known as "the Sarge," Matthews had three hits, including his second homer of the series, and drove in four runs in a 7–2 victory. Rookie Charles Hudson pitched a complete game as the Phillies beat 15-game winner Bob Welch.

Needing one more win to secure the pennant, Philadelphia turned to Carlton again. Lefty's job was easy after Matthews gave him a 3–0 lead with a three-run homer in the first inning. Schmidt chased Reuss with an RBI double in the fifth that put the Phillies ahead 4–1, and Sixto Lezcano hit a two-run shot in the sixth. The Phillies won 7–2 and advanced to the World Series for the second time in four years. Schmidt batted .467 (7-for-15) with one homer and two RBIs, but Matthews was the NLCS MVP. He hit .429 (6-for-14) with three homers and eight RBIs.

"Gary's a typical member of the Phillies," Schmidt said. "He's a man with a professional attitude. He realizes what's important is the team."

For Matthews, it was redemption after the worst season of his career. He batted just .258 with 10 homers and 50 RBIs in the regular season. "I've been in some hotter streaks, but this couldn't come at a better time," he said. "It really makes me feel good."

Owens felt some vindication after the Phillies vanquished the Dodgers. He brought together a group of older players in the twilight of their careers to go for it all, possibly for the last time, and his gutsy strategy worked. The Phillies were National League champions.

"Nobody gave up," Owens said during a joyous celebration in the locker room. "Even after all the baloney we went through, everybody kept at it. To me, this is a season I will never forget."

Standing between the Phillies and their second World Series title were the Baltimore Orioles, a team rich in pitching with two superstars in the lineup. The Orioles won 98 games during the regular season under first-year manager Joe Altobelli, who replaced the legendary Earl Weaver. They beat the Chicago White Sox in four games to win the AL pennant and advance to the World Series for the second time in five years. The Orioles lost to the Pittsburgh Pirates in the 1979 Fall Classic.

Baltimore's pitching staff was anchored by left-handers Scott McGregor (18–7) and Mike Flanagan (12–4). Rookie right-handers Mike Boddicker (16–8) and Storm Davis (13–7) made it the most formidable staff in the majors. The offense was led by veteran first baseman Eddie Murray and shortstop Cal Ripken Jr., the AL Most Valuable Player. Murray hit .306 with 33 homers and 111 RBIs. Ripken batted .318 with 27 homers and 102 RBIs.

The Orioles were slight favorites over Philadelphia to win the I-95 Series, a reference to the highway connecting the two cities. Unlike 1980, the Phillies' trip to the World Series did not generate as much excitement around town. Fans lacked the same enthusiasm for this team. They had a tough time getting excited during the summer because the Phillies were a mediocre squad that struggled for much of the season. Once they ran away with the division in September, fans could not get caught up in a furious pennant chase.

Six months earlier, the 76ers had won the NBA title. The city should have been buzzing about the possibility of winning two major sports championships in the same year, but the atmosphere was dull.

The Phillies took Game 1 of the series at Baltimore's Memorial Stadium. Joe Morgan, who finished a dismal season with a torrid September, hit a tying homer off McGregor in the sixth inning and Garry Maddox hit a solo shot in the eighth to give the Phillies a 2–1 victory. John Denny was outstanding for 7⅔ innings, allowing only Jim Dwyer's homer in the first. Holland slammed the door shut to secure the win.

Mike Boddicker baffled the Phillies with an assortment of junkballs and pinpoint control in Game 2. The rookie hurler held Philadelphia to three hits and gave up just one unearned run in a 4–1 win that evened the series. Schmidt was 0-for-4 for the second straight game, an ominous sign for a streaky hitter.

The World Series shifted to Veterans Stadium for Game 3. Owens stunned everyone by benching Pete Rose and putting Tony Perez at first base. Rose called the move "embarrassing," but Owens explained that he wanted to get more offense in the lineup. Steve Carlton faced Mike Flanagan on the mound. The Phillies took a 2–0 lead in the third, but squandered opportunities to add more runs. It proved costly when the Orioles tied it in the seventh off Carlton and scored the go-ahead run in the same inning on shortstop Ivan DeJesus' fielding error. Veteran Jim Palmer earned the win with two scoreless innings in relief, and Baltimore's bullpen was the difference in a 3–2 win. Schmidt was hitless in four at-bats, dropping to 0-for-12 in the Series.

The Orioles jumped on Denny in Game 4, taking a 2–0 lead in the fourth, but the Phillies cut the deficit in half in the bottom of the inning. Schmidt snapped an 0-for-13 skid with a broken-bat single and Joe Lefebvre followed with an RBI double off Storm Davis. Denny helped himself with an RBI single in the fifth to tie it, and Rose delivered a run-scoring double to put the Phillies ahead 3–2. Schmidt ended the inning with a fly out. The Orioles took a 4–3 lead in the sixth and added another run in the seventh. Schmidt came up as the tying run in the eighth and fouled out. At that point, he was just 1-for-16 in the series. Finally, the fans let him have it. They unleashed their boos as he returned to the dugout.

"That was the first time they booed me in the series," Schmidt said afterward. "They put up with me making outs as much as they could and I can understand that. I'm just as disappointed as they are. They're not making it tough on me. I guess I'm making it tough for myself to hit."

The Orioles held on for a 5–4 win and moved within a game of winning the championship. While Schmidt's slump affected the Phillies, Baltimore found a way to win three games without much of a contribution from its top slugger. Eddie Murray was just 2-for-16 in the first four games, and he was tired of hearing questions about his slump.

"I've been going through it my whole life. Mike Schmidt is going through the same thing," he said. "The media keeps bringing it up, so it's difficult to ignore. What do you expect? We're out there doing the best we can and if we don't deliver, you jump in our faces. How would you like it?"

Murray busted out of his slump in a big way in Game 5. He slammed two homers and the Orioles got strong pitching from Scott McGregor to blank the Phillies 5–0 and win the third World Series title in franchise history. "There are a lot of ways to look at it, but the bottom line is they were better than us," Schmidt said.

Schmidt finished 1-for-20 with six strikeouts. He could not have picked a worse time to have a slump. "I was constantly trying to adjust and it almost seemed like they knew what I was thinking," he said. "I tried as hard as I could, but it just didn't work out. I apologize for my performance, but not for my effort."

The Wheeze Kids were broken up soon after the World Series ended. The first player to go was Pete Rose; he was released three days after the loss to Baltimore. Rose hit a career-low .245 in 1983, though he came through with a .344 (11-for-32) average in the postseason. Joe Morgan was released two weeks later and Tony Perez was sold to the Reds in December.

Schmidt hated losing Rose, who helped his career tremendously. But he understood the team had to make a business decision.

"The Phillies had gone a long, long time without being in a World Series until Pete Rose arrived," Schmidt said after Rose's departure. "Pete's been in two of them here. He's also been a great friend of mine. I've accomplished a lot during his time here, and I think a great deal of that success has to do with him. Time marches on. So do careers as well as life itself, and you can't ignore that. I'll be in the same boat one day. God willing, it will be four or five years down the road, but I'll be in the same boat, too."

During Rose's five seasons with the Phillies, Schmidt made great strides as a player and matured as a person. With Rose gone, he was unquestionably the team leader. But the two were very different people, and Schmidt never fully embraced a leadership role.

"Pete lived baseball 24 hours a day," Schmidt said. "That's great, but it's not me. I have other interests. I have a family. I'm a father. I dedicate myself to baseball totally once the season starts. But there's more to my life than baseball."

Schmidt was committed to being a strong role model for children and was actively involved in raising funds for organizations such as the United Way, the Philadelphia Child Guidance Clinic, and the Christian Children's Fund. He knew he could make a positive impact on many lives through his work off the field.

"The Lord has a plan for each one of us and His plan for my life has been a wonderful plan," Schmidt said. "I believe that my obligation for the many blessings He has given me is to live my life as an example for children. If I can affect those lives in a positive way, whether it's something I say, or something I do, or something I give, or just living my life as an example so people can say, 'This guy's a good guy, a family man who knows how to love, how to care for people, how to be humble,' then I believe I have lived up to my responsibility."

10

Fitness Freak

"The more progress he made, the more rehab he wanted. He ended up playing five more seasons, and in the process fell in love with physical fitness. He saw how it could lengthen his career, forestall the aging process, and fuel him with energy— emotional and mental as well as physical."
—Pat Croce

Mike Schmidt walked into Pat Croce's office in 1984 with a chronic hamstring problem, a strained rotator cuff, and a body worn down by the constant pounding of playing baseball every day, many of them on the unyielding Astroturf at Veterans Stadium.

Schmidt left the meeting with a new outlook on exercise that eventually changed his life, prolonged his career, and improved his overall health.

Croce, the fitness-guru-turned-self-made-millionaire, was the conditioning coach for the Philadelphia Flyers at the time and headed a physical therapy company in Broomall, Pennsylvania, when Schmidt was introduced to him by a mutual friend. The two hit it off quickly and formed a lasting relationship.

"Pat became my fitness guru and one of my closest friends," Schmidt said. "He basically rebuilt my body with cardiovascular and weight training, restored the flexibility in my legs, and established a workout routine that I'm still addicted to today."

Schmidt was a little skeptical before he began working out with Croce. But Schmidt turned 35 during the final week of the 1984 season, and though he led the league with 36 homers and 106 RBIs while batting .277, he realized he needed to do something to ensure that he would be physically able to perform at a high level in future years.

"I was feeling my age and the pain from nagging muscle pulls in my legs throughout the year," Schmidt said.

So he put his trust in Croce. It was one of the smartest moves he ever made.

"His body was deteriorating to the point that his career was in jeopardy of being cut short," Croce said. "In his mind, though, he was far from finished with baseball. So we set to work on him. And he didn't retire until 1989."

Fans saw Schmidt as a graceful, nonchalant player who hardly ever dove headfirst like Pete Rose or bled or sweat much on the field. That was the knock against him throughout his career in Philadelphia, which reveres the blue-collar type of athlete. In reality, Schmidt was the total opposite of this perception, especially in the gym.

"Mike Schmidt was a workout machine," Croce said. "He enjoyed pain and suffering so much, had such a consuming passion for conditioning, that I couldn't help but wonder if maybe we had been separated at birth."

Schmidt was a perennial All-Star and one of the best players in the major leagues. But Croce treated him like he was any other client, screaming at him for motivation during workouts. "You ain't Jack Shit!" Croce would shout.

"And he would look at me—the sweat running off him in rivers turning his shirt dark as mud, the veins in his temples thick as lead pencils as oxygenated blood pounded through them—and through a face contorted he would...smile! And ask me for more," Croce said.

Croce called Schmidt "the perfect patient, meticulous and obedient." Schmidt worked out with Croce on a regular basis the rest of his career.

"The more progress he made, the more rehab he wanted," Croce said. "He ended up playing five more seasons, and in the process fell in love with physical fitness. He saw how it could lengthen his career, forestall the aging process, and fuel him with energy—emotional and mental as well as physical."

Schmidt, whom Croce referred to as "Jack" instead of Mike, worked out at the center with 76ers star Julius Erving and other prominent athletes and celebrities in the city. Word spread that Croce was training Schmidt and Dr. J, and others wanted in. Croce went on to become a pioneer in the sports physical therapy industry. Besides working for the Flyers, he was also hired by the 76ers as a conditioning coach and several years later orchestrated the purchase of the team. He was president of the club when league MVP Allen Iverson led the 76ers to the NBA Finals against the Los Angeles Lakers in 2001. Croce stepped down as president after that season to pursue other career opportunities and has written several books, hosted television shows, and served as a motivational speaker.

"I always remind him that the day I walked into his clinic was the beginning of the rise of his empire," Schmidt said. "Actually, he did more for me than I did for him."

* * *

Despite another All-Star season from Schmidt, the Phillies finished fourth in the NL East with an 81–81 record in 1984. The Phillies were in a three-way tie with the Chicago Cubs and New York Mets for first place on July 2 and trailed the Mets by just 1½ games on July 19 before they started freefalling. By September 1, they were 8½ games out. A six-game losing streak increased the deficit to double digits and they finished 15½ games behind the Cubs after losing nine straight to end the season.

Schmidt was the veteran surrounded by a bunch of young players. Len Matuszek replaced Pete Rose at first base. Highly touted prospect Juan Samuel took Joe Morgan's spot at second base. Von Hayes became a full-time player in the outfield along with Glenn Wilson. Samuel was the best of the bunch. He batted .272 that season with 19 triples, 15 homers, 69 RBIs, and 72 stolen bases, but he also struck out 168 times. Samuel made the All-Star team and finished second behind New York Mets pitcher Dwight Gooden in voting for the NL Rookie of the Year Award. Schmidt had a strong influence during the early part of Samuel's career.

"I first got a little taste of Mike in spring training in '83 and just watching him prepare himself, starting in spring training all the way until the season and how he got himself ready," Samuel said. "He knew when he had to be ready. He started getting his stroke down the last week of spring training. Some guys are killing the ball early and then they hit a little skid. Mike was more gradual. He knew what he needed to do at what point of spring training and that was something I learned from him when I came up watching him."

Schmidt tutored Samuel on the finer points of hitting and talked to him regularly about wide-ranging baseball topics.

"Schmitty was the one guy, where a day when it's raining and we're going to hit inside, he would come and pull you aside and say, 'You wanna talk baseball?'" Samuel said. "And we would sit outside in the dugout and talk. He would see my game and tell me what I needed to do and where I needed to improve."

Schmidt had reached a point in his career where he was the wise old man that younger players looked up to and admired. He was the one with the World Series ring, MVP trophies, All-Star Game appearances, and Gold Glove Awards. But he wanted more.

After spending the off-season strengthening his body through Croce's grueling workouts, Schmidt was eager to see how his body responded to the daily grind of playing baseball every day. The results were pretty bad during the first part of the 1985 season.

Schmidt batted just .215 with two homers in April and he continued his struggles in May. Through the first two months, Schmidt had a .215 average, six homers, and 20 RBIs in 44 games. The Phillies were dead last in the NL East and needed to make some changes. Paul Owens had stepped down as manager after the '84 season and John Felske replaced him in the dugout.

In late May, top prospect Rick Schu was called up from Triple-A Portland to play third base in a move the team hoped would increase its offense. Schmidt, who had won nine Gold Gloves already, reluctantly went to first base to make room for the young rookie.

"I'm nervous about moving to first base," Schmidt said. "But if this is what the club wants me to do and if this is what they feel will help, then I'll do it."

Schmidt was concerned that he would have a difficult time adjusting to first base defensively and he was uncertain that Schu would provide more offense than John Russell, Tim Corcoran, and John Wockenfuss, the three players who had been alternating at first base.

"The timing is sort of funny," Schmidt said. "While we're 10 games below .500 and I haven't been performing well defensively, I can't see myself being anything more than adequate for a while. So I'm not quite sure how bringing up an inexperienced right-handed hitter will help. It just might weaken us at two positions. Having said that, I also understand that a lot of people in the organization think Schu is going to be a heck of a player. If he can do the job at third, then maybe I'll play at first for the next three to four years. We'll just have to see."

From a team standpoint, the move made sense. Schmidt was getting older and his range was becoming more limited at third base. The Phillies obviously were going nowhere, so it was an ideal time to see if a young player who had success in the minors could develop into a solid player in the big leagues.

"I'm ready, I've worked hard to get back to the big club, and I'm looking forward to playing," a confident Schu said after his promotion. "Replacing Mike at third puts some added pressure on me, I guess. But it's not like he'll be out of the lineup. All I can do is just play hard like I always did. I feel comfortable playing third base, and I've been swinging the bat pretty well the last few weeks, so I can't wait to get started."

Schmidt made his first start at first base on the road against the Los Angeles Dodgers on May 29. He had a single in four at-bats in a 6–1 loss. Switching positions took Schmidt's mind off his hitting woes. He hit .297 with 27 homers and 74 RBIs after making the move, and finished the season with a .277 average, 33 homers, and 93 RBIs.

The '85 Phillies finished fifth in the NL East with a 75–87 record. It was their first losing season since Schmidt's sophomore year in 1974.

Schmidt made a discovery at the plate in August that improved his hitting significantly. The Phillies were facing Doc Gooden and the Mets. During batting practice, Schmidt purposely swung down and through the ball. He realized he was driving the ball better than ever. Using that approach, he ripped a single in his first at-bat and crushed a two-run homer his next time up.

"I've carried those at-bats with me ever since," Schmidt said later in the season. "I finally realized that I wasn't driving through the ball, I was hitting up on it. I went back to driving it down and waiting on the pitch. The walk is my barometer. When I'm going good, I get one or two walks a game. But I was chasing high pitches, and didn't want to hit my own pitch. Now that I use the downswing, more of my swings result in contact as opposed to foul balls. My strikeouts have gone down and my RBIs and walks have gone up."

From the day he altered his swing until the end of the season, Schmidt batted .331 with 14 homers and 36 RBIs in 163 at-bats. He walked 32 times and struck out 33 times.

"After 15 seasons, I finally felt like a great hitter, a really tough out. A good hitter, not just a dangerous hitter," Schmidt said. "There's a big difference."

While Schmidt recalls the 1985 season as the one where he made the transition across the diamond to play first base, it is best remembered as the year of the wig incident.

On July 1, a crowd of 23,091 came to Veterans Stadium riled up and ready to unleash their fury on Schmidt following the critical comments he made about the fans in an interview published two days earlier in the *Montreal Gazette*.

When the Montreal Expos visited Philadelphia in late April, Schmidt granted *Gazette* writer Peter Hadekel an interview. He made harsh statements about the Phillies fans, saying they are "beyond help" and calling them "a mob scene, uncontrollable." Schmidt also made it known that he would have preferred spending his career playing in another city.

"I'll tell you something about playing in Philadelphia," Schmidt said. "Whatever I've got in my career now, I would have had a great [deal] more if I'd played my whole career in Los Angeles or Chicago, you name a town—somewhere where they were just grateful to have me around.... I can't say spoiled is the right word. They've seen me playing well more than badly. I've achieved excellence in baseball in front of those people. But I make a great deal [of money] and there's a lot of jealous people in those stands. For their ticket prices, they want to see excellence on a regular basis, and I can't do that for them.... In the past, it [booing] affected me. I was [angry], I tried too hard, I couldn't understand it, and felt sorry for myself. But this season, I could care less. I guarantee you that over my career I would have accomplished more without the periods when I tried so hard to do it for these people. Not because I cared so much. It was more, 'I'll show these people.'... I'd like to see some of those golf professionals shoot 72 if there weren't 'Quiet' signs everywhere or if every time they missed a putt the crowd went, 'Boo, you slob, you choked.'"

When the interview was published in the *Gazette* on June 29, the Phillies were on the road playing the Expos. Schmidt's remarks made big headlines in Philadelphia, and everyone wanted to know why he lashed out. Schmidt admitted he "regretted" making those comments, but also pointed out that he did the interview early in the season during a "miserable stretch." He tried to soften his criticism with a longer explanation.

"I know that I am a little too sensitive," he said. "But I do get disappointed with the behavior of Phillies fans when my performance is subpar. How soon they forget some of the good things that have happened. It's easy to play when you're in first place and it's easy to be a fan when your team is winning every day. But every team and every player is going to have their peaks and valleys. Philadelphia is the toughest town I've ever been around when you're in a valley."

Schmidt added that he "hoped the fans don't feel that I'm proud of my .237 batting average. I feel worse about my performance this season than any of the fans. But I can't quit. I've got to keep going out there every day to get out of the slump."

Schmidt also made it clear that he did not want to play anywhere else and hoped to finish his career with the Phillies. "I never want to be traded," he said. "I love my home, my kids are in school and they love the Philadelphia area. I also have friends in town as well as business interests. Our roots are here."

The backtracking came too late for the fans. They arrived at the stadium filled with venom when the Phillies returned. They were eager to make their feelings known. They were angry and hurt by Schmidt's comments. Their only method of retaliation would be to boo him louder than ever before.

"Everyone knew I was in trouble," Schmidt said. "My teammates wouldn't stand near me in pregame drills; I think they were afraid of a sniper. Back in the clubhouse after BP, I walked by Larry Andersen's locker and saw this long, black wig. Larry kept us loose with pranks and costumes, and he was generally the instigator of all clubhouse fun. Just for a laugh, I put it on. Then Steve Jeltz gave me his Porsche sunglasses and—presto!—I had a disguise. I could go on the field incognito.

"But the guys started ragging me, saying I had no guts, daring me to do it, saying the fans wouldn't know what to do if I went out in that getup. So, scared out of my mind, I went with it. The fans freaked out. They'd come for blood, at least some of them, and at first they seemed dumbfounded—and they started to laugh and cheer. I guess it showed them I wanted to acknowledge the tongue-lashing I'd given them, and to show them a human side of me they'd never seen."

The crowd booed lustily when Schmidt's name was announced during pregame introductions before the Phillies played the Chicago Cubs. They kept booing until Schmidt ran out of the dugout to take his position at first base still wearing the wig and sunglasses. Suddenly, the boos turned to cheers and applause as Schmidt took warm-up tosses in his disguise.

After Schmidt struck out his first time up, he heard boos again. But this time they were the typical jeers—the ones without malice. Schmidt got two hits in his next three trips to the plate. He came up again with two outs in the bottom of the ninth and the Phillies trailing 3–1. There were two runners on base and Cubs closer Lee Smith was on the mound. The hard-throwing Smith fired a fastball past Schmidt, striking him out to end the game. Schmidt walked back to the dugout with the familiar refrain of boos ringing in his ears.

"I have more respect for Mike Schmidt than any other hitter in the league," Smith said, defending his opponent. "This man is at the top of my list. Even when he doesn't hit the ball good it can go out. He wears me out in Wrigley Field."

The wig incident changed some fans' perception of Schmidt. They started to realize that maybe Mr. Cool had a sense of humor and a down-to-earth side after all. Schmidt would hear boos again in his career, but the image of him running on the field in a long wig and dark sunglasses goes down as one of the most memorable and light-hearted moments in his career.

"I think he finally realized that he's a great player, and maybe when he came out in the wig, I think that was him saying, 'If they want to boo me, I'm fine with it,'" said former teammate Larry Bowa, who played for the Cubs that night. "He spent a lot of his career worried about perception, what people thought of him, what the writers thought of him, and that wears you out."

Juan Samuel still laughs when he thinks about seeing Schmidt warming up in that Halloween disguise.

"I didn't think he was going to do it. I really didn't think he would go through with it," Samuel said. "He was expecting to be booed. But he showed he had a sense of humor. He had a dry sense of humor sometimes."

* * *

Mike Schmidt hardly got a chance to break in his first baseman's glove before he had to put it away and head back across the diamond to his familiar spot at third base.

After compiling their worst record in 12 years, the Phillies were determined to become a contender again in 1986. They revamped their lineup in the off-season by acquiring outfielders Gary Redus and Milt Thompson in separate trades. Von Hayes moved from center field to first base, Schmidt went back to third, and Rick Schu took a seat on the bench. Schu had a decent two-thirds of a season as a rookie, but he drove in just 24 runs in 416 at-bats and committed 20 errors.

Redus and Thompson were expected to upgrade the offense and help solidify the defense. With Redus leading off, Thompson batting second, and Juan Samuel hitting third, the Phillies had more speed atop their lineup than ever before. That meant plenty of opportunities for Schmidt to knock in some runs. At 36 years old, Schmidt still was showing no signs of slowing down. Considering how well he hit during the final six weeks in '85 after changing his batting approach, Schmidt had grandiose plans.

For the first time since the early 1970s, the Phillies were rebounding from a losing season, and expectations were tempered in spring training.

There was a mood of confidence among the players and they genuinely felt comfortable around each other, but no team since the 1961 Cincinnati Reds had finished as many as 26 games out and came back to win a title the next year. At least the Phillies had more experience on their roster after fielding three rookies in the Opening Day lineup in 1985.

"I think we genuinely like each other on the club, and when we talk about the team with each other, we all say that we could be a really good club," Schmidt said in spring training. "We're going to have to be a team that communicates, that has that so-called chemistry. We haven't proved we're a contending club and we have some questions to be answered. That's why we'll need to be together, and I feel that very strongly right now. And it will help that this year we won't have anyone out there who'll be walking into the Vet for the first time. Everyone's been around enough not to have inexperience be an excuse. There are always concerns at every position and this year is no exception. But being around this group of players, I'm becoming more and more optimistic about the kind of team we can be."

The biggest question mark for the Phillies was pitching. Steve Carlton was trying to rebound from a career-threatening shoulder injury at age 41. Behind him, Shane Rawley and Kevin Gross were top-notch starters. But after them, the Phillies were counting on youngsters to step up and fill out the rotation.

"In my mind, our season comes down to how our pitchers perform and how we play defense," Schmidt said. "We're going to score runs.... You can talk all you want about clutch hitting and game-winning home runs. But we have to prove we can win those games that depend on you doing the little things, like turning the double play at the right time, or a reliever coming in and stopping that tying run from scoring. In every season, there are probably 55 games you're going to win and 55 games you're going to lose, no matter what. So your success comes down to those 50 games that can go either way. And those are the games where defense and pitching play the biggest role."

Schmidt did not hit a homer in spring training, but picked up where he left off the previous season once the games started to count. He batted

.330 in the first 25 games, but the Phillies were only 10–15. They were already 10½ games out of first place by May 10 because the New York Mets got off to a blistering 20–4 start.

The Mets stayed hot and easily ran away with the division. The Phillies finished strong after a rough first half. From August 1 until the end of the season, they went 37–25 to finish in second place with an 86–75 record. The Mets won 108 games en route to beating the Boston Red Sox to win their second World Series title.

Schmidt hit .290 and clubbed 37 homers to earn his eighth home-run title. He also drove in 119 runs to win his fourth RBI crown. After the season, Schmidt was voted National League Most Valuable Player for the third time in his career. He became just the third player in the NL to win the award three times, joining Stan Musial of the St. Louis Cardinals and Roy Campanella of the Dodgers. Four American League players—Jimmie Foxx, Joe DiMaggio, Yogi Berra, and Mickey Mantle—had also won it three times. Barry Bonds, Alex Rodriguez, and Albert Pujols have since joined the group.

At 37, Schmidt was the second-oldest MVP in history. Willie Stargell was 39 when he shared the award with Keith Hernandez in 1979.

"This has been the most enjoyable season of my career because of the warmth, the encouragement and respect coming out of the stands, especially after so many years of highs and lows," Schmidt said as his voice cracked during a news conference in Philadelphia. "That's the thing I'll remember and cherish the most about the 1986 season."

Schmidt received 15 of 24 first-place votes in the balloting by the Baseball Writers Association of America. Glenn Davis of the NL West champion Houston Astros finished second. Gary Carter and Hernandez, who both played for the World Series champion Mets, came in third and fourth, respectively. Carter thought players that helped their team reach the postseason were more deserving of winning the MVP Award.

"I've always been told that it would be a player on a winning team," Carter said.

Hernandez had no complaints because "the Mets won the big award."

"I'd have voted for Mike Schmidt, too," Hernandez said. "He put up great numbers and is deserving. He was the most valuable player this year. No player on the winning teams stood out with great statistical years. Anybody else besides Schmidt who thought they had a chance was only fooling themselves."

While other players his age were retiring or trying to play with declining skills, Schmidt proved he was still at the top of his game. Asked if he thought he should be MVP, Schmidt emphatically said, "Yes."

"This feels something like the end of a political campaign the way the voting broke down," he said. "I feel like a political candidate making his acceptance speech after months and months of campaigning."

While celebrating his award, Schmidt said he might play just one more season and then retire. He cited family obligations and concern that his children—eight-year-old Jessica Rae and six-year-old Jonathan—needed him to be around the house more.

"Since the season ended, my thoughts are basically the same," Schmidt said. "I'm not looking past next year. I went to school and talked with my little boy's teacher. He's having a problem right now with my career. He's in the first grade. That's a concern of mine, his growing up and being able to be normal, one of the kids. And the longer I continue to play as he gets older the tougher it's going to be for him…to be Jonathan Schmidt as opposed to Mike Schmidt's little boy. That's going to carry weight in my decision.

"Can I slowly get out of the headlines and the limelight? I don't want to do it in a declining career and have to be told, 'You've played enough.'"

Later in the news conference, Schmidt said, "At this point in time I'm convinced I have one more year of active play in this body. And that's the way it's going to stand."

But he did leave open the possibility he would change his mind and play beyond 1987.

"If my knees are okay, if my wife and family can cope with another year or two and the club is a contender," he said. "But unless I fall flat on my face next season I want to go out on top. I've invested and done well and I'm able to leave."

Before he left the podium, Schmidt reflected on his achievement and took satisfaction in his extraordinary accomplishment.

"Since my last MVP in 1981, there have been some valleys," he said. "I had some good years and some so-so years. There were some hard times. People were questioning whether I could still cut it at third base. And there was some talk that it was time to trade Mike Schmidt. So to rebound to this level at the age of 37 is quite gratifying. Because the end of my career is near, there is much more pressure to do well, to go out on top. For both of those reasons, this is a very special thing for me."

CHAPTER

11

The 500 Club

*"Swing and a long drive…there it is…
No. 500, the 500th career home run for
Michael Jack Schmidt, and the Phillies have
regained the lead at Pittsburgh 8–6."*
—Harry Kalas

S pring training was a media circus for Mike Schmidt in 1987. He was just five home runs shy of the elite 500-homer club, and many baseball writers from across the country wanted to discuss the pending milestone with him.

Every morning, Larry Shenk, the public relations vice president for the Phillies, gave Schmidt a list of the visiting writers who wanted to speak to him. Schmidt held daily morning press briefings for 20 to 30 minutes, which gave writers a chance to conduct their interviews and ask the same questions—over and over and over again.

Schmidt did his best to accommodate everyone and answer their redundant questions. He knew that Roger Maris struggled in dealing with the media during his pursuit of Babe Ruth's single-season home-run record in 1961. He also watched how well Pete Rose handled the attention he got when he chased Stan Musial's National League hits record in 1981. All eyes would be on Schmidt now, and he was ready for the pressure.

"I keep telling these guys I don't know [what to expect]," Schmidt said during spring training. "I'm going to make every effort I can to be available and to be congenial and cooperate. The toughest thing for me is toleration for the same questions over and over again."

Schmidt consulted Rose, his good friend, for advice on dealing with the constant scrutiny. Rose told him it would not be easy, but to try and have fun with it.

"For the most part, what I learned from Pete was, first you've got to accept that there's not going to be a lot of free, relaxed, kidding-around time. Any time somebody sees you standing alone they figure it's their turn, it's their time," Schmidt said. "I think if you understand that—and you're never happy with that—but if you understand that's the way people are, if you can build up a callousness toward that sort of thing and give that person the time, and be as congenial as you can to that person and explain there will be another time later in the day...Then you don't lose a lot of friends and you keep a good image of yourself. There won't be any black marks written or anything you're not happy with throughout the whole episode.

"I'm attempting to do that. I watched Pete. I'm trying to make it an event that will be enjoyable for me and be courteous in my own eyes. Sometimes you can tell people about the human interest side of 500 home runs, which I find to be the most interesting part."

Schmidt hoped to hit No. 500 at Veterans Stadium so the hometown fans could share the moment and joy with him. He hit Nos. 100, 200, 300, and 400 on the road. But he had no intention of going out of his way to ensure he would do it in Philadelphia.

"I won't sit out a game on the road if I'm healthy enough to play, or the final at-bat of a game," he said. "Team goals come first. Mike Schmidt's goal is going to come, but not at the expense of playing foolish or selfish baseball. Probably the thing I'm proudest of with the number of home runs I've hit is that I've actually tried to hit so few. If I had been up there looking to hit a homer every at-bat, I'd probably be going after career homer No. 200 by this time—if I was still here."

Team goals were Schmidt's primary concern at that point of his career. He was 37 years old and coming off his third NL MVP season, but he was already thinking of retirement. Schmidt was entering the final season of his $10 million contract and family obligations were becoming a priority. If he left, he wanted to go out on top.

The Phillies had a winning record in 1986, but were never in contention in the division because the New York Mets ran away from the pack. Most baseball experts figured the Mets were not going to win 108 games again. The Phillies had a chance to contend if they could close the gap between the two teams.

Schmidt lobbied hard in the off-season for the team to get another big hitter in the lineup, and team president Bill Giles made a huge splash in free agency to get one. At a time when other owners were unwilling to spend big bucks on players, Giles lured catcher Lance Parrish away from the Detroit Tigers with a one-year contract worth $800,000, plus incentives for another $200,000 if he stayed healthy. Parrish averaged 30 homers and 99 RBIs over his previous four seasons in Detroit and helped the Tigers win the World Series in 1984, but he missed much of the second half in '86 with a back injury. Parrish officially signed with the Phillies on March 13 following lengthy contract negotiations. He immediately was plugged into the No. 5 spot in the lineup behind Schmidt and was expected to provide power and production.

Before signing Parrish, the Phillies had already added Mike Easler to their offense. Nicknamed "the Hit Man," Easler had a career .294 average and gave the Phillies another left-handed bat to complement Von Hayes in the lineup. From top to bottom, Philadelphia's offense had the potential to score a lot of runs. If the pitching held up, the Phillies had a chance.

"We feel pretty, in fact very, confident that we have a chance to win the division and win the whole shooting match, really," Giles said before the season opener. "We think our starting eight is as good as anybody's. The big if, of course, is if our starting pitchers stay healthy."

With Parrish on board and the team's prospects looking up, Schmidt began thinking about playing beyond the season. There was no reason to rush an important decision like retirement.

"Let's face it, playing major league baseball is a very good occupation," he said late in spring training. "It's an easy thing to say this will be my last season. But the final decision will be a very difficult one. It will be tough to say, 'I'm retiring.' I guess it'll come down to what it has always come down to for me. If I feel good about playing physically, if I feel that my family would be best served by playing, then I'll keep playing. And what the club looks like will have a strong influence on my decision. If we're going to be a contender for the next few years, then that would make it a lot easier to stay. So, basically, it's in God's hands. I'm going to go as far as He wants me to go."

The Phillies kicked off the season with four straight losses and were 1–8 heading into a weekend series against the Pittsburgh Pirates at Three Rivers Stadium. Schmidt had three homers in the first nine games, but none of them helped the team win a game.

Before the series opener on Friday night, Schmidt called his wife because he had a feeling his historic homer could happen in Pittsburgh.

He needed just two more to reach it. "If you want to see my 500th home run, you'd better fly out to Pittsburgh," he told Donna on the phone. "I can't guarantee that I won't hit it, and I know I'll be disappointed if you weren't here."

Despite battling a virus that had also stricken the couple's two children, Donna Schmidt left the kids in her mother's care, packed her bags, and got ready to fly to Pittsburgh on Saturday morning.

On Friday night, Schmidt connected off Bob Patterson leading off the second inning for No. 499. The Phillies went on to win 6–2 in 10 innings. Schmidt had four chances to hit No. 500 that night. He flied out, popped out, grounded out, and was intentionally walked.

Donna arrived at Three Rivers Stadium on Saturday afternoon just in time for Schmidt's first at-bat. He popped out to first base against former teammate Bob Walk. Schmidt walked his next time up and scored on Parrish's three-run homer to give the Phillies a 5–0 lead.

Facing Logan Easley in the fifth inning, Schmidt flied out to left field. He flied out again off Brian Fisher in the seventh. The Pirates rallied against reliever Steve Bedrosian in the eighth, taking a 6–5 lead on Johnny Ray's three-run homer.

That set the stage for Schmidt to come up with the game on the line in the ninth. Pinch-hitter Greg Gross grounded out leading off the inning. Milt Thompson followed with a single but was erased on Juan Samuel's fielder's choice grounder. Samuel stole second with Von Hayes at the plate and went to third on a wild pitch. Hayes then drew a walk to put two runners on for Schmidt.

On the mound for the Pirates was Don Robinson, a former starter who had been converted into a closer. Robinson's first pitch missed outside and his next two offerings were low. Schmidt stepped out of the batter's box before the 3–0 pitch. He had the green light to swing if he wanted to, and he knew Robinson probably would challenge him with a fastball. All the Phillies needed was a single to tie the game and avoid what could be a devastating loss.

"I'm standing there thinking, *I've got to get relaxed. Get 'home run' out of your mind,*" he said. "I knew we didn't need a home run to win the game, just a single. I knew if I got a good pitch to hit on 3–0, I was going to try and hit a line drive."

Schmidt stepped back in the box, took a deep breath, and waited for Robinson's pitch. Legendary Phillies broadcaster Harry Kalas made the call:

> "Swing and a long drive…there it is…No. 500, the 500th career home run for Michael Jack Schmidt, and the Phillies have regained the lead at Pittsburgh 8–6."

Schmidt crushed Robinson's fastball an estimated 360 feet over the left-field wall. The stoic slugger uncharacteristically displayed some emotion after his shot sailed out of the park. Schmidt shuffled his feet and did a little high-step dance on his way toward first base as teammates burst out of the dugout to celebrate the moment.

Juan Samuel, who was standing on third base, had never seen Schmidt so excited.

"I saw a little side of him that I didn't ever see before," Samuel recalled. "You never saw him do things like that, 'pimp' a home run like we call it now."

Phillies bullpen coach Mike Ryan retrieved the ball and presented it to Schmidt in the dugout. Schmidt knew he could not have picked a better time to hit No. 500. The Phillies desperately needed to avoid another loss, especially after blowing a 5–0 lead. Kent Tekulve held the Pirates scoreless in the bottom of the ninth to secure the win, and Schmidt was called upon to play shortstop for the final three outs.

"I don't know who wrote that script, but whoever did deserves the Pulitzer Prize," Schmidt said after exchanging a postgame kiss with Donna. "I'm elated, what can I say? It all happened so fast. Of those guys on the 500-homer list, you would be hard-pressed to find one who hit a home run with a better storybook ending than that."

Before Schmidt walked to the plate to face Robinson, manager John Felske almost predicted it.

"How could you ask for a better time for that homer?" Felske said afterward. "We were all talking about it on the bench before he hit it, what a time it would be for No. 500. Everybody on the bench was excited as they could be."

Schmidt had just a .123 batting average against Robinson before he took him deep in a clutch spot.

"I'm sure he didn't want to walk me there because that puts that winning run on second base," Schmidt said. "Robinson's a battler, he's a tiger and he's going to challenge you. He's had pretty good success against me, but today I got him."

Schmidt became the 14th player in major league history to hit 500 home runs and he was the sixth player to hit Nos. 499 and 500 in consecutive games. Babe Ruth, Ted Williams, Willie Mays, Frank Robinson, and Eddie Mathews also accomplished that feat.

"What will I tell my grandkids when they ask me about No. 500?" Schmidt said, repeating a question. "I'll tell them I pointed to left field before I hit it."

Robinson, who was nicknamed "the Sheriff" by teammates because he had a reputation for being a fierce competitor, was upset he surrendered the milestone homer to lose a game.

"If we had been ahead 5–0, 5–1, it wouldn't have been so bad, but this cost us the ballgame," he said. "I came in and blew it. It's as simple as that. We had a great rally and I blew it on one pitch. I knew as soon as he hit it that it was gone."

Joining the 500 club put Schmidt in elite company. Only four players reached 500 home runs in fewer official at-bats than Schmidt, who did it in his 7,331st official trip to the plate. Babe Ruth (5,800), Harmon Killebrew (6,671), and Mickey Mantle (7,300) did it in fewer at-bats. Only two players did it in fewer seasons than Schmidt, who reached the total in his 16th year. Willie Mays needed 14 seasons and Hank Aaron got there in 15. Only four players did it in fewer games than Schmidt's 2,118. They were Ruth (1,740), Killebrew (1,955), Jimmie Foxx (1,971), and Mays (1,987).

"Over the course of my career, I've found more enjoyment in adjusting, trying to figure out better ways to produce more runs," Schmidt said. "I never, ever, ever was home-run oriented as a hitter. My whole career, I fought the desire to hit home runs, to swing for home runs. I always had to fight that, and fight it, and fight it. Every time I'd break down and swing underneath a ball, I'd back out of the box and realize what I'd done, and that's why I'd fouled a ball off or struck out. It was that urge to pull the ball to left field and hit a home run that did it."

Schmidt's teammates marveled at his accomplishment. Lance Parrish was second on the team in career homers and he had 213, almost 300 less than Schmidt.

"That kind of puts it in perspective," he said. "Five hundred home runs to me is just unbelievable."

Von Hayes trailed Schmidt by more than 400 homers at that point.

"It's unimaginable," he said. "As a teammate of his, I try not to even think about things like that, because I don't want to get into a situation where you're intimidated by your own teammate."

Schmidt had always prided himself on being a complete hitter. He wanted to hit line drives and bat .300 more than anything else.

"For most of my career, the home runs were a hell of a lot easier to hit than the singles to right field," he said. "I almost felt like I was more of a threat if it took a home run to win a game than if it took a single. I could hit those home runs. If you had told me in the beginning of my career that I was going to play 17, 18 years, I would have said I'd hit my 500th home run somewhere around 1990. It was simple mathematics.

"I only hit 18 my first year. But then I hit 36-38-38-38. So I had an idea what it took to get 35 homers. But I would never have told you I was going to get 3,000 hits. From my own standpoint, it would take a hell of a lot more concentration and discipline to get 3,000 hits—let alone 4,000 like Pete Rose has got—than it takes to get 500 home runs. Now, I'm sure the singles hitters would tell you that the 500 homers is harder. But it's the guys who have 3,000 hits and 500 homers who are awesome to me."

Hank Aaron and Willie Mays were the only players in the 3,000/500 club in 1987. Eddie Murray and Rafael Palmeiro have since joined that exclusive fraternity.

Schmidt changed his hitting style twice in his career. First, he adopted the off-the-plate, back-in-the-box, swing-easy approach that was similar to Robert Clemente's technique. He won MVP Awards in 1980 and 1981 hitting that way. Then came the adjustment he made in August 1985—holding his bat up high and swinging down—which led to him winning the MVP Award in 1986 and having perhaps his best all-around season. That second tweak was a reaction to an influx of power pitchers in the mid-1980s.

"I could possibly be the last guy to ever do it," Schmidt said after joining the 500 club. "And one reason is that the science of pitching today compared with the styles of hitting is not conducive to long careers or high home-run totals."

Schmidt was way off in his prediction. When Gary Sheffield of the New York Mets connected for his 500th homer in April 2009, he became the 25th player to reach that milestone.

Soon after Schmidt hit No. 500, the tough Philly fans started showing him more appreciation. Perhaps all his talk about retirement made them realize he might not be around much longer, or perhaps they finally understood that he really was among the all-time greats.

"I think they've always accepted that I'm a good ballplayer. I think they've accepted me as one of the better ballplayers," Schmidt said. "But I think that all the publicity surrounding that 500th home run, that number and all that's written about that—how long it takes to get there and stuff—that's had an effect. I mean, I think I got there faster than anybody other than Mays. And when you start telling those Philadelphia fans that one of their own players, one of their own kind, one of the guys they've lived and died with for 10 years, is doing something like that, they start comparing him to Babe Ruth, Hank Aaron, Willie Mays, they sit back and go, 'Wait a minute. No kidding? Right in front of my own eyes he was doing that? I didn't know that. I was too busy booing him.'"

After hitting his 400th career homer against the Dodgers in Los Angeles, a writer asked Schmidt if he thought he would have had a different career playing somewhere other than Philadelphia and he answered, "Yes, definitely."

One hundred homers later, how did he feel about that comment?

"There are two ways to look at that. But the best way for me to look at it is that the highs and lows that I've had in front of the Philadelphians have been a learning experience for me that made me a better player," Schmidt said. "They've brought the best out in me over my career. Who knows what effect the St. Louis crowd that doesn't really get into the game much would have had, what kind of player I'd have been in front of them? Who knows what kind of player I'd have been in L.A., in front of a crowd that seems like they could really care less what happens.

"There's been pressure my whole career to play well in front of the Philadelphia fans. And as much as I might have said back around my 400th home run that had I been relaxed my whole career and had been able to just let it happen and not have the ill effects of booing I might have been a greater player, now as I look back, I think playing in Philadelphia was probably the best thing that ever happened to me."

* * *

With Schmidt's milestone homer out of the way, the Phillies went back to business. They were 3–8 and needed to climb out of an early hole. Schmidt started the series finale against Pittsburgh, but did not put a ball in play. He struck out three times and walked once in a 5–2 loss.

The Phillies were not living up to their expectations and manager John Felske was under the gun. Schmidt created quite a stir with his mouth in mid-May when he ripped the entire organization from top to bottom.

"My one overriding goal is to do whatever it takes to help get this Phillies organization back on top," he said. "I don't necessarily mean on top of the National League East. On top in terms of scouting, player development, the minor league system, the clubhouse, the field.

"We've gone from having the best of everything. We were the Dodgers of the National League East, the Dallas Cowboys of baseball, to what I consider rock bottom. Rock bottom, maybe that's a little bit harsh. We're not polished anymore. The minor league system is depleted. The front office has a little to be desired in terms of positions that are held and the jobs they're doing.

"I'm asked about my goals. The field is the worst field in the league. The dugouts are filthy. The clubhouse is dirty. The pride factor is not what it used to be. We used to have the best field, now it's the worst. We used to have the cleanest dugouts, now they're the dirtiest. We used to have the best minor league system...

"In the next four or five years, as long as I'm young enough and healthy enough, my goal is to make a difference somewhere, to leave the game of baseball with an organization that's back on top."

Later that day, Schmidt reinforced his remarks by pointing out stains in the tunnel from the clubhouse to the dugout at Veterans Stadium. "Cat stink," he said to reporters.

Management did not appreciate Schmidt's stinging criticism and stadium employees made it known they were unhappy with his candid remarks. When Schmidt arrived in the clubhouse for the next game, candles surrounded his chair and green ferns were hanging in his locker. Workers mockingly scrubbed the runway between the clubhouse and the dugout to eliminate the supposed cat stench.

The controversy eventually passed as winning games remained a bigger concern than playing in a pleasant environment. By late May, the Phillies were 17–23 heading into a nine-game road trip to the West Coast. In the first game at San Diego, Schmidt pulled a rib cage muscle and was forced to go on the 15-day disabled list. Rick Schu filled in for Schmidt and the Phillies went 9–4 during his absence. They were at .500 (27–27) when he returned to the lineup June 10 against St. Louis. He went 5-for-10 upon returning, but the Phillies lost three straight games.

On June 14 against the Expos at Olympic Stadium, Schmidt belted three homers, drove in six runs, and helped the Phillies avoid a three-game sweep in an 11–6 victory. Three games later, Felske was fired with the Phillies at 29–32 and 9½ games out of first place. He was replaced by Lee Elia, who was a former manager of the Chicago Cubs and someone who served in the Phillies organization for several years.

Under Elia, the Phillies went 51–50 and finished 80–82, far below their high expectations. Schmidt had another All-Star season, hitting .293 with 35 homers and 113 RBIs. He struck out just 80 times, a career-low except for the strike-shortened season in 1981.

It was an ideal time for Schmidt to go out on top. But he simply could not retire when he was still one of the top hitters in the game. All he needed now was a contract to return for another season.

CHAPTER 12

Moody Mike

"He would come in sometimes and not even say hello to anybody and we'd be like, 'What's wrong with him?' It was all about performance to him. If he wasn't doing well, it would stay with him."

—Juan Samuel

Mike Schmidt was six minutes away from filing for free agency when his representatives, Arthur Rosenberg and Paul Shapiro, agreed to a $4.5 million, two-year contract with the Phillies at 11:53 PM on November 9, 1987.

The deadline filing may have been a mere formality, but Phillies president Bill Giles wanted to avoid letting Schmidt test the open market. The team's representatives and Schmidt's agents negotiated furiously for 10 hours to beat the deadline and finally settled on acceptable terms. Only the first year of the contract was guaranteed. Schmidt would receive $2.25 million in 1988 with $100,000 being donated to a charity of his choice. The contract called for several incentives should Schmidt win another MVP Award or finish in the top five in voting for the award. Schmidt would get paid another $2.25 million if the team wanted him back in 1989, but he would receive only $350,000 if the Phillies released him.

Giles lavished Schmidt with praise at a news conference announcing the deal. He raved about Schmidt's exemplary lifestyle and lauded his performance on the field. Giles certainly was not ready to envision a Phillies team without No. 20 playing third base.

"It would be disheartening to me to have a man who has played here for 15 years and done so much to have to become a free agent and go to arbitration," he said the day after the agreement was reached. "It's just not the right thing, in my mind, to do for a man who has meant so much. And besides, there was always a slight chance that somebody might come along and make him an offer he couldn't refuse, too. I was 99 percent sure that he'd play here and we'd work it out. But I just didn't want to read in the paper this morning that Mike Schmidt was a free agent."

The superlatives flowed out of Giles' mouth that day. He called Schmidt "the greatest third baseman that's ever played this game" and "maybe the best player that's ever played this game." Just two months earlier, Giles was far less complimentary in his assessment of Schmidt. Late in the season, Giles had publicly questioned Schmidt's leadership skills.

"I'm thoroughly convinced our biggest problem is in the head, in the emotions," he said, referring to Schmidt. "He's intelligent enough to be a leader, but he's so moody."

Given a chance to respond to that statement and armed with a new contract, Schmidt chose instead to take the diplomatic approach.

"They're looking at the ideal situation," Schmidt said. "They would hope I would do what I do on the field, which is their No. 1 priority, and be Pete Rose off the field. Moody is probably not that far off in terms of describing me. However, I think we all have that label at times. I think Giles is [moody], and I know Bowa was. I think they're looking for the ideal mood every day, and there's not a player around that has that."

Schmidt made many adjustments in the physical way he played the game, particularly changing his batting stance and his approach at the plate. He constantly tinkered and tried new things. Now in the latter stages of his career, he was thinking about adopting a new mental outlook.

"I think I've got to take a good hard look at my role as the leader on the ballclub, consider some kind of adjustment in that area," he said. "I've talked many times about what I want to do different going into a year. I always seem to mention, 'Geez, I'd like to be more emotional.' I'm totally satisfied with myself in terms of my behind-the-scenes leadership, my approach to the game, my leading by example. But maybe I have to pat a few more butts and do a little more screaming in the clubhouse, and maybe be a little more verbal. You know how I am. I sit kind of quiet and I get my game face on and I start thinking about my own problems and get into my own thing. I play kind of a quiet, subdued game, and at the end of the year it looks pretty good. If you had a bunch of guys doing it like I did, you'd have a championship team."

Schmidt spent some time chatting with younger players about hitting and other nuances of the game, but he was not the type of person who would offer encouragement or lift their spirits with compliments.

"Now that I look back on it, maybe I'm not enough of a positive influence on people," he said. "I can name three or four guys that I am a positive influence on. But maybe Chris James and Von Hayes and Milt Thompson aren't enough. Maybe a little less talk about how to hold your bat and how you stride and a little more talk about the positives would help.

"Most of the [young] players on the team are a little scared of me. I've done my best to try to ease the pressure of that situation. I've been out to dinner with every kid on that team. Still, it's human nature. Ten years ago, if I were playing with Hank Aaron, I'd be thinking, *I've got to watch what I do, what I say.* Maybe the best in these young guys isn't coming out."

Juan Samuel was one of the young players who took a back seat to Schmidt. Samuel had a spectacular season in 1987, his fourth full year in the majors. Sammy batted .272 with 28 homers, 100 RBIs, and stole 35 bases while earning his second trip to the All-Star Game. Giles and others in the front office thought the affable Samuel was perfectly suited for a leadership role. But he was reluctant to accept the responsibility, deferring instead to Schmidt.

"I remember one time I was called in to the office with Bill Giles and a few other people and they asked me to be more of a vocal leader because they thought we needed that," Samuel recalled. "I remember telling them, 'As long as Schmitty is here, I can't do it. How can I do it? I'm only 20-something years old.'"

Samuel said players never knew which Schmidt they were getting on a daily basis because of his mood swings.

"He would come in sometimes and not even say hello to anybody and we'd be like, 'What's wrong with him?'" Samuel said. "It was all about performance to him. If he wasn't doing well, it would stay with him."

At 38 years old, Schmidt figured he would try to be more cheerful, more outgoing, and a little less moody.

"I can work on making myself better in that area, in hopes that it would help the team," he said. "I mean, maybe I force myself to come to the ballpark with a little more happy-go-lucky, how-you-doing-today smile and talk to everybody. Then they'll probably start talking about what a great leader I was."

Dallas Green had tried unsuccessfully to get Schmidt to enjoy himself more and be less introspective.

"I really talked to him about showing emotion," Green said. "I said, 'You gotta enjoy a game-winning three-run home run or a walk-off hit or a big home run in your career.' I said, 'You gotta enjoy that, Schmitty. We do.' I've been in baseball for eons and people love to see that. I said, 'You should just show that to the fans. I don't want you to fake anything because that's not you, but it's also not you to just run around the bases like nothing happened. You should enjoy the moment of baseball and what you just accomplished.' We kept talking about it and talking about it and he just kept saying, 'That's the way I am.'

"I said, 'There's nothing wrong with you being you, but I just wish you would enjoy the game more,' and he would try once in a while and show a little bit of emotion, but he kept that as a guarded thing throughout his career. You see what he did after hitting the 500th homer and that's probably as much emotion as you ever saw out of Schmitty."

Now, finally, Schmidt was seriously thinking about becoming a vocal and emotional leader. He thought about it even more over the winter and reiterated his vow early in spring training.

"I'm so concerned about my own individual performance that I get a little withdrawn sometimes," he said. "Now I'm going to do the best I can to come out of my shell. There's not much left for me to accomplish on the field. So the thing I long for most is to be remembered as a leader of men. So I'm going to try to show a little more emotion. There will be a little less, 'So what, another home run,' after I hit one, although I think that if I batted .250, hit 15 homers, and drove in 50 runs but was a heckuva cheerleader all year there might be a problem."

* * *

Schmidt's new attitude helped create a different atmosphere in the clubhouse during spring training. The mood was lighter and the outlook was positive. In Lee Elia, the Phillies had a manager who was respected by all his players. The coaching staff was filled with excellent communicators who stressed fundamentals. After finishing 15 games out in 1987, the Phillies were hoping to be a contending team.

The offense had the potential to score a lot of runs. The addition of Phil Bradley, a speedy outfielder and career .300 hitter, bolstered the lineup. Lance Parrish had the benefit of a full spring training and was expected to provide some pop after a poor first season in Philadelphia. Schmidt tore the cover off the ball in spring training, hitting close to .500 and showing no signs of his age.

Once again, pitching would be the key. But the Phillies' starting rotation did not compare favorably with the starting staffs of the St. Louis Cardinals and New York Mets. The bullpen also had issues because closer Steve Bedrosian, who won the National League Cy Young Award in '87, was injured and unavailable for the first month.

The Phillies opened the season at Veterans Stadium against the Pittsburgh Pirates. Schmidt homered and had two hits, but his error led to three unearned runs in a 5–3 loss. Schmidt homered again the next night in an extra-inning victory and the Phillies reeled off three straight wins. But then they lost seven in a row and things started to fall apart.

By mid-May, the Phillies were 12–21 and already 10½ games out of first place. Schmidt was hitting just .207 with five homers and 22 RBIs at the end of the month. He also was having a tough time in the field. The media and fans started questioning his skills, and Schmidt understood their concerns.

"There should be questions about me," he said. "Am I a DH now? Am I starting to decline? I wouldn't deny that. Hey, it's human. It's human nature for me to be concerned. I'm concerned enough to wonder whether this is the big one."

Schmidt's bat speed had slowed. His range in the field was more limited. He no longer ran the bases with the same aggressiveness. Even nagging injuries were taking longer to heal, a normal obstacle for older players. Everything else, including the travel schedule and the daily grind, had become a hassle. Schmidt seriously started to wonder if he should have retired and ended his career on a high note.

Early in the summer, Schmidt started experiencing pain in his right shoulder. Unwilling to sit out, he kept playing and hoped it would eventually get better. He finally went on the disabled list in August, thinking some rest would allow him to return before the end of the season. A few days before his scheduled return, Schmidt took batting practice and felt weak. He chose to have more therapy and never made it back to the field that season. Schmidt finished with a .249 batting average, 12 homers, and 62 RBIs in 108 games. It was his worst statistical year since his rookie season.

The Phillies were flat-out awful in 1988. They finished last in the division at 65–96. Only the Atlanta Braves, who were 54–106, had a worse record in the National League.

To make matters worse for Schmidt, his rotator cuff was in bad shape. The team physician recommended major surgery. Retirement was another option. Schmidt chose to get a second opinion from Dr. James Andrews, a renowned sports orthopedic surgeon in Birmingham, Alabama. Andrews suggested an arthroscopic procedure.

"This sounded a hell of a lot better than slicing my shoulder open, so I returned soon thereafter for the procedure," Schmidt said. "Shortly thereafter, with the help of a therapist, I moved my right arm through its full range. The post-surgery pain is indescribable. The traumatized area doesn't want to move right away, but because of the arthroscopic procedure, which did not require an incision, you can still move it. The six-month rehab, with the goal of returning to the Phillies, was my inspiration."

Schmidt was determined to come back, but the Phillies were not so sure bringing him back for another year was the best idea. The team declined to pick up the option on Schmidt's contract that would have paid him $2.25 million. Instead, they offered him a contract that included $300,000 guaranteed plus another $1.4 million in incentives.

Schmidt rejected the deal out of pride and opted for free agency. The greatest third baseman in team history now was available to any team that wanted to pay him. The problem for Schmidt was that major league owners were not willing to pay players big money at the time.

"To the Phillies and 25 other 'colluding' teams, I was damaged goods," Schmidt said. "Sure, I'd been injured, and I had surgery. But many players had similar surgery, recovered, and returned to form. Why shouldn't I?"

Some teams expressed interest in Schmidt, but only the Cincinnati Reds made him an offer. Pete Rose was managing the Reds and he knew Schmidt could still play. Schmidt, however, wanted to finish his career in Philadelphia, even though he was unhappy with management over contract negotiations. He eventually agreed to an incentive-laden contract that guaranteed him $500,000 with the possibility of earning a total of $2.05 million. Despite some bitterness, Schmidt was happy to be back.

"I had a very good understanding of the Phillies' position with me," he said. "I mean, I kind of stand out like a sore thumb on this ballclub— in terms of what I'm making, in terms of my age, in terms of the way the organization is planning to go the next two or three years, in terms of what they could get for me as free-agent compensation if I did sign with somebody else. I could have wound up in another city. I could have ended up not playing anywhere. There were a lot of things on the downside of these negotiations that were different than the other ones. But in the end, I think the issue of loyalty was the real reason I ended up back where I wanted to be the whole time, anyway."

Once again, Schmidt talked about leadership, his relationship with his teammates, and his public perception.

"I don't know if I can ever change people's images of me," he said. "I can't change my career—what I've accomplished, what I've done. I'm a family man. I'm a clean-living man. The way I play, I try to be an example to kids. And I probably want more than anybody in the Phillies organization to win—more than Bill Giles, more than the owners, more than anybody.

"But maybe I'm at fault for that. Over the years, in the many times I've been interviewed, I've told the truth—as I see it. And that probably has hurt a few people, including myself, from time to time. I've got to contain those opinions now. I've got to be a little more concerned about those kinds of things. I see that now. I've learned a lesson."

Schmidt spent the next several months working out vigorously and rehabbing his shoulder so he could prove all the doubters wrong.

Schmidt was medically cleared to play in February and went to spring training eager to test his shoulder. He was the main focus for the media throughout the spring. Many questioned his health and whether he had anything left.

"Everyone kind of likes to be a prognosticator of sorts," he told the *Tampa Tribune* that spring. "It would give people a lot of joy to see me fail, so they could tell other people, 'See, told you he couldn't make it back.' That's what people are waiting for. If you're associated with the Philadelphia media or town, you look for negatives. That's just the way it is. I don't know if there's something in the air or something about their upbringing or they have too many hoagies, too much cream cheese, too much W.C. Fields, I don't know what it is. But they're always so pessimistic. I'll be damned if I let that get a grip on me and what I'm trying to do. I want to have the chance to leave on my terms. I'm goal-oriented, and that's one of them.

"I'd love to have a great season and have [everybody] come to me and say, 'Mike, please stay,' because that's when I'd leave."

Despite his confidence, Schmidt was a realist. He and his wife discussed retirement in the off-season. The possibility that he could become the fourth player behind Hank Aaron, Babe Ruth, and Willie Mays to hit 600 career homers was a small incentive to keep playing, but he would not stay active solely for that reason.

"At the end of the year when I look down at my knees and see the scars, and the wear and tear on my shoulder, and weigh that against my wife wanting me [to be home]," he said. "We kind of talked about this in terms of one more year. I think she's looking forward to me being at home, having more of a normal life, not having the pressure of being on this ballclub and all that entails.

"You already know what this spring has done in terms of pressure on me and her, and on our lives. That's something I can get rid of by not being a player. I'm looking forward to a career outside of baseball, or in baseball in another [capacity].

"Hitting my 600th home run is so far down the list of priorities for me, it's ridiculous. It's way behind my family, and my wife, our love, health, happiness. Six hundred home runs is way down the list."

Considering he was still recovering from the surgery on his shoulder, it was no surprise Schmidt struggled that spring. New manager Nick Leyva faced daily questions from reporters about the aging star. Youngster Chris James outplayed Schmidt in the spring, but there was no competition for the job. Schmidt had earned the right to be the starter, even if he was nowhere close to being the same player anymore.

Moving Schmidt back to first base to take pressure off his healing shoulder seemed like an obvious decision, but that was not an option because the Phillies wanted promising prospect Ricky Jordan to play every day at first.

"If this were a situation of two kids going for the same job, Chris James would have beat him out," general manager Lee Thomas said. "But that isn't the situation. A veteran player cannot be judged on spring training."

Thomas and Leyva knew Schmidt was not going to hit 35 homers or knock in 100 runs, but they hoped he could still be a productive player in the middle of the lineup. Schmidt's shoulder bothered him more in the field than it did at the plate, so he thought he would still be able to hit well.

After failing to hit a home run in spring training, Schmidt connected off Chicago Cubs reliever Calvin Schiraldi on Opening Day. He hit another homer the next day and had five hits over the following two games. But it was all downhill from there. The end was very near.

CHAPTER

13

Hangin' Up the Spikes

*"Some 18 years ago, I left Dayton, Ohio,
with two very bad knees and a dream to
become a major league baseball player…
I thank God the dream came true."*
—Mike Schmidt

Mike Schmidt fielded thousands of ground balls in his life and turned countless double plays, winning all those Gold Glove Awards along the way. But it took just one error for him to realize that it was time to call it quits.

The Phillies were playing the San Francisco Giants at Candlestick Park on May 28, 1989. The score was tied at 3–3 with the Giants batting in the bottom of the fourth inning. With runners on first and second and two outs, Robby Thompson hit a grounder to third base that should have ended the inning. Instead, the ball scooted between Schmidt's legs and into left field to load the bases.

Will Clark came up next and crushed Mike Maddux's pitch over the fence for a grand slam to give the Giants a 7–3 lead in an otherwise meaningless game. As Clark rounded the bases, Schmidt made his decision. This would be his last game in the major leagues.

Schmidt knew if he could no longer make a simple play on a routine grounder that it was time to walk away from the game. He had been agonizing over that decision, praying daily for direction and hoping for a sign to help him make the right choice at the right time. When Thompson's grounder rolled under his glove, Schmidt figured that was his sign. It was time to go.

Schmidt was 39 years old and struggling to play the game at the high level he was used to playing it throughout his career. He was batting just .203 with six homers and 28 RBIs in 42 games. He had eight errors in the field, and simply playing every day had become a chore. It was no longer fun for him to even be at the ballpark. The Phillies were buried in last place in the National League East and going nowhere. He was sick of losing.

It is never easy for a professional player to retire from the sport he loves, but Schmidt wanted to do it with dignity. He felt he was becoming a burden on new manager Nick Leyva, who gave him the support a player of his stature deserved. He did not want to linger too long like so many other superstars did before him. He watched Steve Carlton struggle through his final three seasons, bouncing around the majors and playing for five different teams. Schmidt was determined to leave on his own terms.

Having made the decision final in his mind, all that was left was to finish the game, knowing that it would be his last. Schmidt grounded out to short his next time up in the fifth inning. In the seventh, he hit a slow roller that shortstop Jose Uribe botched. The play was initially ruled a hit and later changed to an error. Schmidt came up again in the ninth against reliever Mike LaCoss and walked. When he reached first base, he told first-base coach Tony Taylor that he was done.

"I was thinking, *Who do I tell first? My wife? The owner? The general manager? A friend?* It turned out to be Tony Taylor," Schmidt said. "When I got to first, I looked at him and said, 'You've just seen my last at-bat.' He looked at me like, *Are you crazy?*"

Taylor thought Schmidt was kidding, but quickly realized he was serious. "I said, 'No, no, no. Don't do it,'" Taylor said. "I was more than surprised. I was shocked. I never expected him to do that. I knew he was still a great player."

Schmidt called his wife Donna and his agent after the game. He informed Leyva of his decision before boarding the team plane to San Diego. He told the rest of the traveling party and his teammates on the plane. The players were stunned to hear the news and some tried to convince Schmidt to keep playing.

"I tried to tell him to wait until the end of the season," said center fielder Juan Samuel, who temporarily replaced Schmidt as the cleanup hitter in the lineup. "I said, 'Why are you doing that? You are going to leave us naked. We have a few more months to go. Finish the season.' But that last series in San Francisco was hard on him. That did it. I said, 'Schmitty, things might get better.' But I guess nobody knows yourself better than you. But I wish he could've stayed with us and finished that season."

Samuel himself did not even finish the year with the Phillies. He was traded to the New York Mets in a multiplayer deal that brought Lenny Dykstra to Philadelphia one month after Schmidt retired. Dykstra played a major role in helping the Phillies win the NL pennant in 1993.

After Schmidt informed everyone on the team plane about his decision, some of the veterans planned a small party for him at a hotel in San Diego. Samuel skipped the party because he thought it would be too emotional.

"I didn't go because I didn't want to see it end," recalled Samuel, who coached third base for the Baltimore Orioles during the 2009 season. "I didn't want to see him like that and see the tears."

Catcher Darren Daulton, closer Steve Bedrosian, outfielder Von Hayes, and many others gathered in a hotel room to bid Schmidt's great career farewell and to celebrate with their friend.

"I'll never forget it," Schmidt said. "As the players filtered in, each of them hugged me and shared a private thought related to our friendship. My closest friends—veterans like Daulton, Bedrosian, Hayes, and Chris James—shared tears with me. There's no stronger emotional bond than to have another man hug you and tell you he loves you."

The next step was making his retirement public at a news conference on Memorial Day. Schmidt dreaded the moment. Two hours before the Phillies played the Padres at Jack Murphy Stadium, Schmidt stood before a microphone in a vacant football locker room and tearfully announced his retirement.

"Bear with me on this, because this isn't easy," he began. "Over the years of my career, I've set high standards for myself as a player, always said that when I don't feel I could perform up to those standards, that it would be time to retire. My skills to do those things on the field, to make the adjustments needed to hit, to make the routine play on defense, and to run the bases aggressively, have deteriorated.

"I feel like I could easily ask the Phillies to make me a part-time player, and to hang around for a couple years, to add to my statistical totals. However, my respect for the game, my teammates, the fans, won't allow me to do that. For these reasons, I've decided to retire as an active player."

Schmidt fought back tears and continued his speech, thanking the Phillies organization, his teammates, and the fans. He paused several times to compose himself while reporters, team officials, and many of his teammates looked on in the crowded room.

"You probably won't believe this by the way I look right now, but this is a joyous time for me," he said. "I've had a great career. My family and friends and I are very content and excited about my decision. It's the beginning of a new life focus.

"Some 18 years ago, I left Dayton, Ohio, with two very bad knees and a dream to become a major league baseball player..."

At that point, Schmidt started sobbing.

"I thank God the dream came true."

Schmidt was crying so hard he had to step away from the podium. Team president Bill Giles came forward and took the microphone.

"Thank you from the bottom of my heart, and for all the Phillies fans who have seen you play over 16 years," he said to Schmidt. "In my opinion, you're the greatest third baseman of all time. It's been a real honor and pleasure to have seen you play over 7,000 hours of baseball in a Phillies uniform."

By retiring during the season, Schmidt walked away from a lot of money. He could have earned another $800,000 that year, but money was not his motivator. He had too much pride to stick around.

"You could see in his face that he wasn't happy," Leyva told reporters. "It was completely different from the way he was early in the year when things were going well. This man has a lot of pride. He just felt it was his time, and I respected that. He just feels he's not doing the job anymore."

Schmidt made sure he spoke to his teammates the night before his news conference because he did not want them to think he was quitting on them when they were struggling.

"Quit is a word I don't want associated with my name," he said. "I told them a lot of good things could happen. Guys are going to get to play every day."

Pete Rose thought his good friend would have kept playing if he had signed that free-agent contract with the Reds during the off-season.

"I hate to see him retire," Rose said. "He hasn't gotten off to the kind of start he wanted to. I still think he would have been better off coming here. I think Mike needs to be on a good team, a team that has a chance to win."

Broadcaster Richie Ashburn had the same feeling.

"Some athletes never want to quit. Some keep going because they need the money; you have to drag them away from the game kicking and screaming," he wrote in his column for the *Philadelphia Daily News*. "Some retire because they can't produce anymore. Some retire because they lose interest. I know one thing: Schmidt doesn't need the money.... I don't know for sure about his ability to produce on the baseball field; he hasn't done much lately. But if the Phillies were serious contenders, I have the feeling Schmidt would have contributed more. It is painfully obvious that Schmidt was agonizing over his hitting and his fielding. And over his lack of interest.

"So, Mike Schmidt's playing career has ended with hardly a whimper in a flurry of poor fielding and weak hitting. But he won't be forgotten easily, and it is quite likely that a baseball player of his ilk never will pass this way again."

Schmidt conceded that the standings were a factor in his decision, though he stressed it was not his team's fault he chose to retire.

"It's hypothetical, but if [we were winning], I wouldn't have had all this mental anguish. And I probably wouldn't have retired," he said.

The timing was terrible with the Phillies being on the West Coast, about 2,700 miles away from home. The setting was surreal. No one could ever have envisioned one of baseball's all-time greats announcing his retirement in a football locker room that was used a day earlier by the Beach Boys for a postgame concert.

But Schmidt had always done things his way. Once he explained his decision, everyone understood.

"That the best player in the history of the Phillies' franchise announced his retirement in a football locker room in San Diego in May in the middle of a road trip will forever live as the ultimate Schmittyism, the final non sequitur," wrote *Philadelphia Daily News* columnist Rich Hoffman. "But listening to him, it made sense. Hearing the words and seeing the emotions that burst through a dam that had been so solid for so long, it made sense. He had been too good for too long. He had been too good to accept what he had become. And so, he left."

Around the majors and across the nation, people stopped and offered their praise for Schmidt, the player and the person.

"I admire Mike. I have nothing but a lot of respect for him," Hall of Fame third baseman Eddie Mathews said. "He's my type of person; I know him well enough to say that. As he started breaking all my records, I viewed him as the kind of guy I would want to do it."

Hank Aaron called Schmidt a "tremendous ballplayer" who "comes along once in a lifetime."

"He is one of the best players and one of the best athletes I've ever seen. He has achieved so many great things," former Phillies manager Dallas Green said.

Schmidt's opponents also showed their admiration.

"For a power hitter, he knew the strike zone better than anybody," Nolan Ryan said. "I could never get him to chase a bad pitch."

Former teammates expressed sadness to see him go.

"I was concerned that people would perceive him as having quit," Garry Maddox said. "That's one word you cannot use to describe Mike Schmidt. I think back to the times I played with him. There are different types of leaders. Mike was the type where you knew the best chance the team had of winning was with him in the lineup. He would go out time and time again with injuries and that allowed everyone else to play to the best of their abilities."

One day after his emotional speech in San Diego, Schmidt had to do it again back home in Philadelphia. Standing at home plate at Veterans Stadium, Schmidt held another news conference with the local media. This one was not tearful; rather, it revealed more insight about the man Schmidt really was. He always came across to fans and the media as a laid-back, confident person, but deep down he was insecure like so many others.

"I longed to be a great major league baseball player and have people want my autograph," he said. "I wanted all the things young players want. But I wasn't sure I had the confidence. I wasn't sure I was man enough to do that. I wasn't sure I could do the things I needed to do to stay in the big leagues, to be one of the Philadelphia Phillies forever. I really wasn't sure.

"I'm no different than any person who undertakes something in their life that scares them. Of course, the macho feeling, the ego within me wouldn't allow that to surface. I walked around like a cool guy, like a guy who was sure of himself, like nothing bothered me. That was not the case. I was very unsure of myself and probably a little scared."

When the Phillies returned home from the West Coast later that week, Schmidt returned to the Vet to say farewell to the fans before a game against the Atlanta Braves. With video highlights of his career playing on the big screen in center field, Schmidt walked to the microphone as flashbulbs flickered. The crowd gave him a loud standing ovation, showing their appreciation.

"None of us have any control over the future in our lives," he said. "All we can do is dream and hope that God allows us to fulfill our dreams. God allowed me to fulfill my dream.

"I thank you people for being a very, very large part of that dream. The noise you made over the years, the great sounds of approval and those ugly sounds of disapproval, are all part of a career, are all a single part of the whole. And I thank God you were here to be part of my career, to push me to the limit. Thank you so much. God bless you all."

Schmidt made history that summer by becoming the first retired player to be voted into the All-Star Game. He joined the rest of the National League All-Stars for the game at Anaheim Stadium, but declined to play. After all, Mike Schmidt was retired and finally at peace with himself.

CHAPTER

14

Call to the Hall

"At the time Mike Schmidt was voted into the Hall of Fame, I don't think there was much argument that he was the best third baseman who ever played."

—Paul Hagen

They came by the busloads, more than 200 of them filled with Phillies fans wearing their red caps, T-shirts, and No. 20 jerseys. They packed their lawn chairs and their beach towels and made the nearly five-hour trek from Philadelphia to upstate New York to visit the quaint village of Cooperstown, the home of the National Baseball Hall of Fame Museum.

A charming town located on Lake Otsego, Cooperstown has a population of only 2,000 or so residents within its 1.6 square miles, and there is only one stoplight in the entire town. But for one weekend every summer, Cooperstown comes alive as baseball fans flock there from all across the country to attend the Hall of Fame induction ceremony.

On July 30, 1995, Phillies fans turned Cooperstown into a sea of red. An estimated 28,000 people, mostly from the Philadelphia area, descended upon the tiny village to see two of their heroes receive the greatest honor that can be bestowed upon a major league ballplayer.

Mike Schmidt and Richie Ashburn were inducted into the Hall of Fame that day. It was only fitting that the greatest player in team history and perhaps the most beloved sports figure the city had ever known were linked together in such a special way.

Schmidt's selection to the Hall of Fame was a foregone conclusion. Long before he retired in 1989, Schmidt had earned his place among baseball's elite superstars alongside Babe Ruth, Mickey Mantle, Hank Aaron, Willie Mays, and many others. His career numbers clearly put him in an exclusive category with the best of all time: three Most Valuable Player Awards, 10 Gold Glove Awards, 12 All-Star Game selections, and 548 career home runs.

Ashburn, known affectionately as "Whitey" to his legions of fans, never was a clear-cut choice for the Hall. He was a career .308 hitter and an excellent defensive center fielder who made the All-Star team five times during his 15-year career with the Phillies, Chicago Cubs, and New York Mets. He had 2,574 career hits; no player in the decade of the 1950s had more hits than Ashburn. But his road to Cooperstown was a long one, and it included plenty of campaigning on his behalf and from his many supporters. Ashburn did not receive the required number of votes from the baseball writers to gain entry into the Hall, but he finally was elected by the Veterans Committee.

To qualify for the Hall of Fame, a player has to be retired for five years and must have played at least 10 seasons in the major leagues. A screening committee eliminates candidates with lesser qualifications before they are presented on a ballot for eligibility. Members of the Baseball Writers Association of America who have been part of the organization for at least 10 continuous years have the privilege of voting players into the Hall of Fame. A player has to receive at least 75 percent of the votes to be elected. Players who get less than 5 percent of the votes are dropped from consideration. Every player who gets more than 5 percent stays on the ballot for a maximum of 15 years, providing they continue to get at least 5 percent.

Players who are passed over by the writers still have a chance to get in if they get the required percentage of votes from the Veterans Committee. For much of its existence, this committee consisted of 15 members selected by the Hall of Fame for defined terms. It was later revised in 2001 to consist of living members of the Hall of Fame, winners of the Ford Frick Award for baseball broadcasters, and winners of the J. G. Taylor Spink Award for baseball writers. Election procedures were changed in 2003 and again in 2007.

When it came time for Schmidt's name to appear on the Hall of Fame ballot for the first time, the only question was whether he would be the first unanimous choice in history. On January 9, 1995, Schmidt was elected to the Hall with an overwhelming 96.5 percent of the votes. He was named on 444 of 460 ballots. Sixteen writers, for whatever reason, did not deem him worthy on his first try. At the time, only Tom Seaver, Ty Cobb, and Hank Aaron had ever received a higher percentage of the votes. Nolan Ryan, Cal Ripken Jr., George Brett, and Tony Gwynn have since earned a greater percentage.

Two months later, the Veterans Committee elected Ashburn. There would be no more debating over his credentials. Ashburn joined baseball's exclusive fraternity 33 years after playing his final game.

Schmidt has some issues with the voting system because he feels politics and personal bias play too much of a role in the process. Some writers will not vote *any* player in on the first ballot, no matter how worthy his resume. Others may let their own personal feelings about a player determine their vote. A player who was friendly with the media during his career could get the benefit of the doubt over a player who was difficult to deal with or reluctant to grant interviews.

"I don't mind baseball writers having personal feelings about players. I have personal feelings about writers," Schmidt said. "But when they let personal feelings unrelated to on-field performance influence their votes for the Hall of Fame, I do have a problem. A big problem."

Paul Hagen, a longtime baseball writer for the *Philadelphia Daily News*, was among the vast majority of voters who concluded that Schmidt was an obvious choice.

"At the time Mike Schmidt was voted into the Hall of Fame, I don't think there was much argument that he was the best third baseman who ever played," Hagen said. "He was a complete hitter who just happened to hit 548 home runs in an era when that was even more of an accomplishment than it became later. He was a Gold Glove defender, a three-time Most Valuable Player. I'm sure the handful of people who failed to vote for him had their reasons, but if you don't cast a ballot for the best player ever at his position, I'm not sure what the criteria for a Hall of Famer is."

Schmidt's solution is to have the original vote by the writers serve as a preliminary vote. Players who qualify would then be reviewed by a smaller committee of voters who would have the final say. His proposed committee would consist of distinguished, senior members of the BBWAA nominated and elected by their peers.

"This panel would function much like a jury, weighing the evidence before returning its verdict," Schmidt said. "I feel this would flush out the politics and the personal bias and allow a player's qualifications to be judged on their merits."

* * *

On Induction Day, it was a time to celebrate instead of debate. Schmidt was joined in Cooperstown by his wife Donna, daughter Jessica, son Jonathan, his parents Lois and Jack, and his sister Sally. On the night before the ceremony, then–club president Bill Giles threw a private party for Schmidt and Ashburn. Family, friends, and former teammates, including Hall of Fame pitcher Steve Carlton, and former Phillies owner Ruly Carpenter attended the gathering.

By Sunday morning, thousands of Schmidt's well-wishers had arrived to share in the celebration. Cooperstown was transformed into a smaller version of the City of Brotherly Love; so many Phillies fans made the 265-mile journey, it became the largest crowd in the history of the Hall of Fame. A total of 9,700 people visited the Hall's museum on July 29, and another 8,424 walked through the doors on Induction Day. Those figures represented single-day attendance records that stood until 2007 when the museum drew more than 14,000 visitors when Tony Gwynn and Cal Ripken Jr. were inducted.

It was a hot and sunny Sunday in Cooperstown, perfect weather for Phillies fans who usually spent beautiful days like that watching a game at Veterans Stadium or relaxing at the Jersey Shore. They set down their chairs and blankets on the lawn, covering the green grass with red-and-white pinstripes. Some of the spectators were so far from the stage they could hardly see the inductees. Giant video screens all around the complex allowed fans in the distance to stay tuned into the festivities.

In the weeks and days leading up to the ceremony, a hot topic around Philadelphia centered on the possibility that fans might not give Schmidt a completely warm reception. After all, Schmidt's relationship with the people in Philly was sometimes stormy during his career. Just weeks before his induction, Schmidt criticized the fans and the city in an interview with *Philadelphia* magazine.

"It's hard for me to be positive, to have real good things to say about a town that never did anything for me and, in general, made life miserable for me," he said in the July 1995 issue of the magazine.

Even though he later issued an apology, those were harsh comments that stung fans hard and fueled media speculation that Schmidt might get booed one more time on his day of glory.

A newspaper in Oneonta, New York, even printed this headline the day before the induction: "Phillie fans ready to cheer Ashburn, boo Schmidt."

Schmidt worried about what kind of reception he would get the night before the ceremony. He thought about it some more while he was on stage before his name was called and sought advice from Hall of Famer Reggie Jackson. Schmidt's biggest concern was how he might react to any negativity on such a joyous occasion.

"I was worried and concerned about it," Schmidt told reporters at his news conference after the induction. "Probably more than anything, I was concerned about handling the downside, if there would be some catcalls or some nasty things yelled out at a quiet time."

No need to fret. Phillies fans would not dare ruin this special moment in team history. Despite the bad reputation they have earned for their boorish behavior at times, Phillies fans always seem to know when to rise to the occasion. They came to celebrate a great day with two of their own. Schmidt never was fully appreciated as a player until he retired, so this was everyone's chance to let him know they truly felt privileged to have watched him play all of those years.

The official induction ceremony began with the returning Hall of Famers being introduced on stage. Jackson heard a smattering of boos from the crowd when his named was announced. Then-Philadelphia mayor Ed Rendell heard a few, too. That was it, however. When Ashburn's name was called, chants of "Whitey, Whitey, Whitey" rang out from the crowd at the Clark Sports Center. It felt like home for Ashburn. A generation of fans loved him as a player for his gritty style and hustle. Another generation adored him as a broadcaster for his dry wit, sense of humor, and unique ability to tell interesting stories on air, usually between pitches. To no one's surprise, Ashburn did not prepare his speech; he winged it as only Whitey could.

"I am so happy to be here today. This has changed my life a lot and my family's life," Ashburn said. "I can't believe the number of people here today from Pennsylvania, Delaware, New Jersey. You people aren't here because they're having fireworks tonight or because they gave something away. You're here for the game. I can't believe this!"

Ashburn called it "a great thing" to be inducted with Schmidt. He became emotional during his speech as he recalled loved ones who died before they could see him make the Hall. Ashburn then finished by thanking all the fans in attendance, telling them "you have made this the greatest day of my life!"

The appreciative crowd roared, giving Ashburn a loud ovation. Once they quieted down, it was Schmidt's turn to be introduced, and he got a rousing ovation from the flock of Phillies faithful.

Unlike Ashburn, Schmidt came ready with a carefully prepared speech. Schmidt looked out at all the red-clad fans before him and was overwhelmed by their incredible support. The same fans who booed him when he struck out in clutch situations only to cheer him when he hit home runs came to share his special day.

"What a great day! I only wish that all of you out there could stand right here and see what I am looking at. It's truly amazing!" he said. "You have stretched the city limits of Philadelphia all the way to Cooperstown."

Schmidt congratulated his good friend Whitey and the other inductees—Vic Willis, Leon Day, and William Hulbert. Taking a moment to soak it all in, he marveled at the occasion.

"I really do stand before you as a man that is truly humbled by the magnitude of this entire experience," he said. "It's unbelievable! To be honored at this historic annual baseball ritual is truly the finishing touch on what was an extremely rewarding career."

Schmidt acknowledged everyone who helped him reach this grand stage. There was his grandmother who "used to pitch me a tennis ball in the backyard" when he was a kid. Of course, his parents and wife and children deserved thanks for all their love and support throughout his life and baseball career. He singled out many others, including his college coach, Bob Wren, and Tony Lucadello, the scout who signed him for the Phillies. He mentioned teammates, managers, owners, and others who made it possible for him to become a Hall of Fame player. One person Schmidt gave special thanks to was former teammate Pete Rose, who was banned from the sport for life in 1989 by then-commissioner A. Bartlett Giamatti for gambling on baseball.

Rose declined to attend the ceremony because he did not want to take any attention away from Schmidt. Whenever Rose showed up to an event, he was the main attraction. So he made sure to stay far away from this important day for Schmidt.

"Someday soon I hope Pete Rose will be standing right here," Schmidt said, as the fans cheered in approval. "I know y'all agree with me on that one. It's great that we see eye-to-eye on something, isn't it, Philadelphia?"

With that perfect transition, Schmidt took the opportunity to address his love-hate relationship with the Philly fans. He even put the blame directly on himself.

"If I had it to do all over again, the only thing I would change is me," he said. "I'd be less sensitive. I'd be more outgoing. I'd be more appreciative of what you expected of me."

Hoping to make peace, Schmidt asked the crowd to leave the past issues behind and move forward.

"My relationship with Philly fans has always been misunderstood," he said. "Can we put that to rest here today? My family and myself sure hope we can. Sure there were tough nights and tough games at Vet Stadium. You've got to realize that that's the nature of the sport we play. But I remember most your cheers of anticipation as I would come to the plate for a big at-bat, the curtain calls after big home runs, and that No. 20 being hung on the outfield wall at Vet Stadium forever. And that's the bottom line. Just like today, you're here. Back then, you were there, and I know you cared. For that, I thank you."

The loyal Phillies fans cheered loudly again, letting Schmidt know they had already put all those negative issues behind them and wanted to fully embrace him. Schmidt earned a lot of praise for his speech, particularly the classy way he connected with the fans and made a point of burying the hatchet.

"The whole day called for him to show at least a little personality, and he did, and it registered," recalled Ted Silary, a longtime sportswriter for the *Philadelphia Daily News* who covered Schmidt's induction for the newspaper. "Throughout his career, wasn't that the one thing Phillies fans wanted him to display? The whole undercurrent of 'Will anyone boo him?' was amazing. I guess the media would have gotten back to it, and focused on it, even without Schmidt's cooperation, but he really played into it and acknowledged his fears, concerns, and took us with him in that direction."

After mending fences with the fans, Schmidt turned his attention to the current state of baseball, which needed serious fixing at that time. The 1994 World Series was canceled the previous year because of a labor disagreement between the players and owners, and the current season started three weeks late. Schmidt expressed concern that too many players no longer considered it a "privilege" to play the game and instead were "taking that privilege for granted." He felt some players lacked humility and respect for the opponent and were more interested in their own self-image. He challenged the players and owners to find common ground and to restore baseball's integrity.

"Our game has reached a crossroads," he said. "I don't believe it can survive unless the team owners and players become one. Take a look at the empty seats in the stadiums, or drive by an empty playground where kids used to be playing ball. That concerns me. And, baseball, that should scare you."

Schmidt concluded his speech with a message to children.

"Never stop chasing your dreams. Your dreams are your best motivators," he said. "My career is an example of how you can beat the odds, an example of how someone's dreams can come true. Remember this: in the final analysis, you can believe in your dreams, you can be taught, supported, motivated, and loved by others, but ultimately your success depends on you. You must take responsibility for your body, for your mind, and your character."

After the ceremony, Schmidt, Ashburn, and the other Hall of Famers returned to the Otesaga Hotel on the southern shores of Lake Otsego to pose for the traditional induction weekend group photo. Before the members left their seats, Robin Roberts requested a photo with his fellow Phillies Hall of Famers. That picture of Roberts, Carlton, Schmidt, and Ashburn was enlarged into a wall-sized portrait that now greets fans in the Hall of Fame Club level at Citizens Bank Park. Often fans stop and pose for a picture in front of the portrait with their heroes in the background.

Some people had reservations about Schmidt and Ashburn being inducted together. Each deserved his own day, they argued. But for all those who were there the weekend Phillies fans painted Cooperstown red, it could not have worked out any better.

"Beforehand, part of me felt that it would have been neat for each guy to go in separately so they'd get their individual time in the spotlight, but once we all got there and experienced the great sea-of-red atmosphere, it was impossible not to see it as a stroke of incredibly good fortune," Silary said. "Schmidt appeared to truly appreciate seeing what it meant to Ashburn. In fact, even if he had not been inducted with Whitey, and had just been there as an observer, I'm guessing he still would have said it was one of the best weekends of his life."

Schmidt's plaque in Cooperstown reads: "Unprecedented combination of power and defense with unusual mixture of strength, coordination, and speed made him one of the game's greatest third basemen."

Many consider Schmidt the best to ever play the position. The top challenger for that title is Alex Rodriguez, who was a seven-time All-Star shortstop before he moved to third base after joining the New York Yankees in 2004. Rodriguez had 583 homers entering the 2010 season and was only 34 years old at the time. If he stays healthy, Rodriguez has a chance to break Barry Bonds' career record of 762 homers. But A-Rod's reputation took a severe hit in February 2009 when he admitted that he used steroids earlier in his career as a member of the Texas Rangers.

Once considered a certain first-ballot Hall of Famer, Rodriguez may be kept out of Cooperstown—at least temporarily—because of his steroid use. Other players who have been accused of juicing or were caught during baseball's Steroid Era—Bonds, Mark McGwire, Roger Clemens, Rafael Palmeiro, Sammy Sosa, and Manny Ramirez among them—also are Hall of Fame worthy, based strictly on their numbers. But many baseball writers will be reluctant to vote them in because of the steroid allegations.

McGwire became a prime example in 2007 when he received only 23.5 percent of the votes in his first year of eligibility. McGwire hit 583 home runs and was a 12-time All-Star during his 16 seasons with the Oakland A's and St. Louis Cardinals. He helped revive the game in 1998 when he and Sosa engaged in a thrilling chase of Roger Maris' home-run record. McGwire broke Maris' single-season mark by clubbing 70 homers that year. Sosa finished with 66, five more than Maris hit for the New York Yankees in 1961. Bonds broke McGwire's record by smashing 73 homers in 2001.

In January 2010, McGwire finally came clean and publicly admitted he used steroids on and off throughout his career—including during his record-shattering 1998 season—as he prepared to re-enter baseball as the Cardinals' hitting coach under his former manager, Tony La Russa. His apology confirmed what many baseball writers had long assumed, and it's now quite possible that Big Mac will never be enshrined in Cooperstown.

In 2005, Schmidt thrust himself into the national spotlight when he said he would have used steroids if he was a major leaguer in the 1990s. "Let me go out on a limb and say that if I had played during that era, I would have taken steroids," Schmidt said during a panel discussion on the HBO show *Costas Now*. "We all have these things we deal with in life, and I'm surely not going to sit here and say to you guys, 'I wouldn't have done that.'" Schmidt was criticized by some of the old-timers for his statement, but he was widely applauded for his honesty. One month later, while in Philadelphia to attend a Phillies game, Schmidt backed off his statement slightly. "I'm not saying I definitely would have, but I'm not going to sit here and tell you there's no way," he said. "Who knows? I truly can't make the statement, 'I wouldn't have gotten caught up in it.'"

In his 2006 autobiography, Schmidt changed his stance and said he would not have succumbed to the temptation. "In my research for this book, I have thought long and hard about the use of performance-enhancing drugs in baseball," he said. "I have come to understand how steroid use has spread to the high school and college level. I have reflected on the destructive impact steroids have had on baseball's precious history, its records, and the very integrity of the sport. And I believe in my heart that I would have chosen not to use steroids."

Schmidt has gone back and forth on the issue many times. Just days after Rodriguez admitting using steroids, Schmidt again discussed the topic with reporters when he arrived at the Phillies' spring training complex in February 2009 to serve in his annual role as a hitting instructor. Everyone wanted to know if Schmidt would welcome Rodriguez, an admitted cheater, to the Hall of Fame.

"I'd welcome him if he got elected," Schmidt said. "I always seem to walk down the middle of the fence. I understand the old, hard-line guys that use the word, 'He cheated. He cheated.' And the other guys that go, 'It was a culture thing back then.' If you played back then, you would have been tempted, too. People in glass houses shouldn't throw stones. We've all got things in our closet."

Schmidt was seventh on the all-time home-run list when he retired, but he had dropped to 13th place by the end of the 2008 season, and Jim Thome passed him during the 2009 season. Some of those ahead of Schmidt are linked to steroid use. He does not let it bother him.

"I don't care," he said. "It doesn't matter if I'm 14th. I'm gonna be 30th someday. I'm tired of the whole discussion."

Back in 1998, when McGwire and Sosa were going head-to-head after Maris, Schmidt got caught up in the daily drama just like most fans across America. He admired the players for their abilities and did not consider the possibility that they were cheating.

"I sort of dropped out of baseball in the '90s, besides coming back to Philadelphia once or twice for an alumni function, an honor, or a teammate being honored," he said. "I have to be honest. I was sort of brought back to baseball by McGwire and Sosa, by the home-run chase there. I really got re-energized by the whole thing. I can't say I was watching them going, 'These guys are juiced.' But I was thinking these guys are amazing. Not only are they great hitters, great home-run hitters, they're great entertainers. That was the point in my mind where the persona of the major league baseball player totally changed. They were Ruthian-type entertainers. These guys played to the TV. It's a whole story that's amazing, how everyone was riding the wave. What an exciting time for baseball, home runs and ridiculous numbers and the fans in the ballpark and the revenue and the game's back and man, look how big he got over the winter. That was kind of everyone's attitude."

Eleven years later, Schmidt found himself captivated by a different storyline. He closely followed the situation involving Rodriguez, who was thought to be a clean player during a time when so many other sluggers were suspected of using steroids.

"It's unfortunate," Schmidt said. "These sorts of things have been happening over the last three, four years with various players. A term I think that has been overused a lot, and definitely by Alex, is *culture*. Culture of the era that you played in. We had a culture when I played and a culture in the era when Babe Ruth played. In the '60s, there was a culture. It's that way in life, apparently. In hearing everybody, that was the culture of the mid-'90s and early 2000s and the temptation had to be tremendous for young men playing major league baseball back then. It's part of the evolution of the sport of baseball. It's unfortunate now. It does open a lot of areas for discussion for fans, for the media obviously. You guys are feeding on this. I'm not different. As a fan sitting back, I kind of feed on it, too. I look more at the psychological side of it. How sports fans choose their heroes, how our heroes always seem to let us down. My take on the whole thing, rather than having an Alex Rodriguez as your hero or Roger Clemens as your hero, how about having someone fighting in the war in Iraq or a heart surgeon or Barack Obama? Let's focus more on people that really matter in this world. We tend to build these sports heroes up to a point where they're always going to let us down."

CHAPTER

15

Life After Baseball

"Since my retirement in 1989, I've been haunted by a single baseball question: what would it be like to manage in the major leagues? Something inside has always told me—and still does—that I have what it takes to be a good big-league manager."
—Mike Schmidt

enry Louis Mencken, an American journalist, essayist, and critic in the early 1900s, famously said, "Those who can, do; Those who can't, teach."

This statement can be applied to sports because some of the best managers and coaches were mediocre or below-average players. Connie Mack, Walter Alston, Sparky Anderson, and Tommy Lasorda are Hall of Fame baseball managers who had little success as players.

Early in his career, Mike Schmidt started thinking about becoming a manager after he retired. Back then, it was not unusual for a great player to make the transition to manager. Several Hall of Fame players turned to managing after they stopped playing, including Walter Johnson, Rogers Hornsby, Tris Speaker, Frankie Frisch, Red Schoendienst, Ted Williams, Yogi Berra, and Frank Robinson.

Those Hall of Famers had varying degrees of success as managers. Hornsby, Speaker, Frisch, and Schoendienst won World Series titles; Johnson, Williams, and Robinson never even finished in first place.

Schmidt always figured he would have an inside track to landing a job with the Phillies as either a manager or a general manager. But he never got that chance at the major league level.

When Schmidt retired in May 1989, Nick Leyva was only two months into his first season as the team's manager, Lee Thomas was completing his first calendar year as the general manager, and Denis Menke was in his first season serving as the hitting instructor. The timing was not right for Schmidt then, and Phillies president Bill Giles made it clear that the greatest player in franchise history did not fit into the team's future plans.

"He and I talked last September about managing and batting coach and stuff like that. I just don't think that's in the cards," Giles told reporters after Schmidt announced his retirement on that Memorial Day in San Diego. "I don't think he wants to work in the minor leagues. I think as a player-personnel person, it's not in the cards at all. As a broadcaster, possibly."

Asked why he thought a great player like Schmidt could not be a good teacher, Giles pointed out Schmidt was a unique hitter at the plate.

"I've talked to Lee and Nick about it. They just don't really think he'd be a good hitting coach because his style of hitting was so different," Giles said. "They just didn't feel he would be a good hitting coach. Maybe somebody else would feel differently."

Even before he retired, Schmidt approached Giles about the general manager's job after Woody Woodward was fired during the 1988 season. He was still playing at the time, so Giles did not give it much serious thought. Instead, he chose the more experienced Thomas, who played a key role in the St. Louis Cardinals' front office. Thomas was the director of player development for the Cardinals, helping build a team that won three National League pennants and one World Series title in the 1980s.

Looking to stay involved in the game, Schmidt sought other opportunities after his playing days were over. He auditioned for various broadcasting jobs, including one with CBS. He served as a co-host of the pregame show for the 1989 National League Championship Series and worked the dugout during the games. After CBS acquired the rights for Major League Baseball, Schmidt interviewed for an analyst position but lost out to Tim McCarver and Jim Kaat. Schmidt accepted the Phillies' offer to join their announcing crew on cable television in 1990. He spent one season doing games on the now-defunct PRISM channel before leaving the booth.

"I enjoyed the broadcast, but I wasn't a good fit," he said. "For the most part, my natural speaking voice was too soft and my personality too low-key for TV. I had to be constantly reminded to speak up and put more energy into my voice. I just couldn't fake excitement when a guy singled up the middle, and I got tired of the standard comments like 'I spoke to him before the game' or 'That was a good piece of hitting' that are so common in broadcasts today. I couldn't get comfortable hanging around the clubhouse in my blazer trolling for a sound bite, or in the booth overreacting to what was taking place on the field."

Schmidt wanted to be the man making the calls in the dugout or calling the shots in the front office instead of talking about the action on the field. But Giles did not think Schmidt was cut out for the job.

"Mike is not a people person," Giles said two years after Schmidt retired. "He can appear brusque without realizing it, and that's part of his problem. Communication is a big part of the business, and Mike isn't always a good communicator."

Those comments hurt Schmidt. He was not a phony person who made politically correct statements just to please others. Rather, he spoke his mind. The media demanded answers from him throughout his career and he provided them by saying what he truly felt, even if he stirred up controversy at times.

"Talking to reporters is probably the reason I'm not the general manager," Schmidt said, responding to Giles' criticism. "I'm just not good at editing what I say. I've said a lot of things over the years that ruffled people's feathers, including Bill Giles'. But I said what I said because I care about this organization."

In 1992, Schmidt thought he had found his way back into baseball. He was asked to be part of an ownership group that was pursuing the newly awarded expansion franchise in Florida. Schmidt spent a year traveling back and forth from Philadelphia to Florida, meeting with politicians and community leaders to help develop his group's formal presentation to Major League Baseball. This was an exciting opportunity. Schmidt would get a part ownership of the team and be the general manager. However, Schmidt's group lost out to Wayne Huizenga. Five years later, the free-spending Huizenga guided the Florida Marlins to their first World Series victory.

Meanwhile, Schmidt was still looking for a way back. He briefly sought a career in the sports agency business, working with Rick Horrow, who headed his baseball ownership group. Horrow became the head of Golden Bear International, a new sports management division of Jack Nicklaus' Golden Bear Inc. Schmidt's role was to acquire clients from college and pro baseball. Jason Giambi and Johnny Damon were among the players he contacted. But the business started slowly and the project was put on hold. Schmidt probably would not have lasted long had it continued anyway.

"Think I'm not cut out for TV? Try picturing me standing outside locker room doors waiting on clients," he said.

Schmidt dealt with the rejection and stayed in the Philadelphia area for a few years after his retirement. Then he and his family moved to Jupiter, Florida. Schmidt found that he could live a more private life down south, and the warm weather allowed him to spend more time working on his golf game.

Schmidt first discovered golf when he picked up his dad's 7 iron in the family's backyard at age 10. He enjoyed the nuances of the game, and playing it stoked his competitive juices. Golf became his new passion and he set his sights on earning a spot on the PGA Senior Tour. Schmidt played golf intensely, trying to perfect his swing and hone his skills so he could win a card and compete with other golfers age 50 or older. He never achieved his goal, but Schmidt continued golfing and playing in celebrity tournaments.

"I feel I can play at that level, but the challenge is to play consistently well," Schmidt said about the Senior Tour.

Though he enjoyed playing golf, Schmidt missed baseball. Thirteen years after he took off his No. 20 jersey for the final time, Schmidt was ready to put the uniform on again. All he needed was an invitation from an organization that had shunned him since his retirement. Except for reunions and promotional events, Schmidt rarely was seen around the Phillies.

Ed Wade, who replaced Lee Thomas as general manager in 1998, extended the proverbial olive branch before the 2002 season. Wade wrote Schmidt a letter, asking him to come to spring training to spend a couple weeks serving as a special hitting instructor on manager Larry Bowa's staff. Schmidt jumped at the chance.

"I haven't felt a lot of substance in my life," Schmidt said. "Every day, it's like, what can Mike Schmidt do for the pleasure and gratification of Mike Schmidt?"

Bowa made it clear to his former teammate this was not an offer made only out of courtesy.

"This was not going to be an autograph session," Bowa said. "I had specific things for him. It's important for an organization to include players of Mike's stature and draw on their knowledge."

The Phillies had several young players, including Scott Rolen, Pat Burrell, and Travis Lee, that could benefit from talking to Schmidt about hitting and how to handle the media scrutiny in Philadelphia as well as the sometimes negative reaction from the hard-core fans. Rolen was involved in bitter contract negotiations with the team and had just turned down a 10-year, $140 million contract. The All-Star third baseman had concerns about the organization's commitment to winning and he did not enjoy playing for the fiery and sometimes abrasive Bowa.

When Schmidt arrived in Clearwater for his first day on February 25, 2002, he immediately was put in the middle of the Rolen vs. Phillies saga. Not surprisingly, Schmidt defended Rolen's stance.

"Scott is a very intelligent guy and he sees the Philadelphia town being one that won't afford him an opportunity over the long haul to ever fulfill his desires in terms of being a world championship team," Schmidt said. "I think Scott is taking a very noble stand to turn down that amount of money. I might sign that thing as fast as I could in case I got hit by a car. But if anybody ever got a chance to sit down with Scott Rolen for an hour, they'd love him. He's a man of principle. He's hardworking. He's honest."

Schmidt tutored Rolen, Burrell, Mike Lieberthal, and other players for the next 11 days. He shared tips on hitting and anything else that could help them become better players.

"He's helped me a ton," Burrell said. "I was surprised at how willing he was to help me. Just having him around, listening to what he was saying about his approach, some of the things he went through, some of the things he sees in us, it's awesome. He has a great perspective on other hitters. He helped me and I'm sure other guys, too."

Lieberthal was not sure what to expect when he heard Schmidt was coming to camp.

"I thought he'd be more of a spectator," Lieberthal said. "But he's really informative. Players have been coming up to me and saying, 'Have you talked to Mike Schmidt about hitting?'"

Schmidt enjoyed the work so much it led to discussions about extending his role with the team.

"Without a doubt, it's been great," he said. "Being at this ballpark, I feel like my life has a purpose. It's not all about me. It's a chance to affect the lives of 25 young men."

Before spring training ended, the Phillies announced that Schmidt would join the team during the season for a total of 12 to 15 games. He would spend time with the players when the Phillies were at home and on the road in Florida, and would work with former teammate Greg Gross, who was the hitting coach.

"We were pleased with the contributions Mike made earlier this spring," Ed Wade said. "Mike was very receptive to working for the organization and we are happy we were able to work out this arrangement. He mixed well with the big-league staff and the players. We talked about a number of things, gave him a list of things he could get involved in if he was interested. We talked about spending time in the farm system, scouting. Basically, tell us what you like to be involved in and we'll see what fits."

Schmidt returned to spring training in the same part-time role the following year. He helped close out Veterans Stadium in September 2003 by participating in a memorable, moving ceremony. Schmidt re-enacted his 500th career homer trot and Tug McGraw, who was battling brain cancer, took the mound and pretended to throw the same final pitch he blew past Kansas City's Willie Wilson to clinch the franchise's first World Series title in 1980.

"Everybody's trying to make this like we should all be crying because they're going to tear down the Vet," Schmidt said. "It must not have much significance if they're going to blow it up, right?"

While in town for the festivities, Schmidt told club president David Montgomery he was thinking about returning to baseball on a full-time basis. Schmidt had conversations with the St. Louis Cardinals and Florida Marlins about possible coaching positions, but felt he owed it to the Phillies to give them the first crack at hiring him.

"Since my retirement in 1989, I've been haunted by a single baseball question: what would it be like to manage in the major leagues?" Schmidt said. "Something inside has always told me—and still does—that I have what it takes to be a good big-league manager. I know how to play baseball to win—that's a given—and I have the leadership qualities to motivate 25 young individuals to put all personal priorities aside and play as a team. The question isn't whether I have what it takes but how much I'm willing to give."

Being a major league manager is not as glamorous as it sounds. It is a demanding job filled with enormous pressure and expectations. Some people simply do not have the personality required for this high-profile position. Others are not willing to make all the sacrifices needed to be successful. Managing is time-consuming and draining, mentally and physically. A manager is on call 24 hours a day, seven days a week, all year long.

Having realized no team would just hand him a big-league job without any prior experience, Schmidt finally decided he would try to work his way up the ladder by starting at the bottom. Inspired by the Florida Marlins' victory over the heavily favored New York Yankees in the 2003 World Series, Schmidt took the first step toward finding out if he had what it takes to be a manager.

"The general feeling in baseball seems to be that high-achieving ballplayers don't make good managers because they don't have the patience to work with players with lesser skills," Schmidt said. "Realizing all this, I wanted to prove I was different. My itch was still there, and the Phillies gave me a chance to scratch it."

Schmidt got a call from Ed Wade in the fall of 2003 asking if he would be interested in managing the team's Single-A affiliate in Clearwater. Wade told Schmidt what the job required and gave him some time to think about it. Accepting this job would drastically change his lifestyle.

Schmidt would have to make a strong commitment to the organization for seven months. He would have to put those celebrity golf tournaments on hold and forget about his weekend fishing trips. Baseball would consume his life. That meant sitting through long bus rides, living out of a suitcase, sleeping in hotel rooms, and sometimes eating dinner from a vending machine. The Florida State League is a long way from the majors. There are few luxuries. You have to love baseball and love your job to want to manage in the low minor leagues.

Schmidt discussed the job with his wife and she convinced him that he needed to work every day and keep his mind active. Naturally, he had some doubts.

"Did I have it in me?" Schmidt said. "Could I discipline myself to dedicate the time and effort toward something like this, something as grueling and focused, something that required me to draw on my own experience to help a band of young men build their careers?"

No Hall of Fame player had ever managed in the minor leagues before. Only two inducted Hall of Famers—Yogi Berra and Frank Robinson—had even managed in the majors in the previous 30 years. But if Schmidt ever wanted to get the chance to reach the next level, he had to start somewhere. After careful consideration, he went for it.

"I wasn't sure if I'd be good at deciding when to hit-and-run or pull a pitcher, but I was absolutely confident in my ability to communicate with and positively affect the lives of young men," he said. "I was also convinced that successfully completing this job would dramatically change other people's perception of me, in the event a major league managing opportunity came along."

Schmidt went to Clearwater to meet with Wade and Mike Arbuckle, the team's minor league director. Both men told him the truth about the job instead of sugarcoating the facts. The pay was low and Schmidt's primary responsibility was to develop talent, not to win games. Schmidt never even played at the Class-A level. He had no idea what to expect. Now he was going to start his managerial career there.

"There wasn't really anything about the job that should have been of interest to me, except the challenge it presented," Schmidt said.

The best part about managing the Clearwater Threshers was the environment. The Threshers played in the sparkling-new $28 million Bright House Networks Field, which served as the Phillies' spring training complex. They had a gorgeous field, state-of-the-art workout facilities, and a locker room so big they only needed to use half of it. There was also a practice field named after Schmidt and another named after Richie Ashburn.

Schmidt's coaching staff consisted of pitching coach Steve Schrenk, hitting and third-base coach Manny Amador, and first-base coach Dan Roberts. Arbuckle and Bill Dancy, the director of minor league camp, assembled the roster, which included only five or six legitimate prospects.

One of them was Cole Hamels, the 17th overall pick in the 2002 amateur draft. Hamels had the potential to be a dominant pitcher if he could just stay healthy. He was 6–3 with a 1.34 ERA and 147 strikeouts in 101 innings in his first year in the minors in 2003. Hamels impressed scouts and wowed everyone watching by pitching two scoreless innings against the New York Yankees in a game that spring. In one inning, the lanky left-hander struck out Derek Jeter, Alex Rodriguez, and Tony Clark in order.

But Schmidt only had Hamels for a short time; the young phenom missed the first month of the season with left elbow tendinitis and was shut down after making four starts. Watching Hamels pitch made Schmidt's job exciting. Other tasks, such as cutting players and disciplining them, took a toll on Schmidt.

Early in the season, Schmidt had to release young catcher Edgar Cruz. It was the first time he had to tell a player to pack his bags, and Cruz's situation made it difficult. Cruz and his wife were expecting the couple's first child any day. That meant Cruz would be an unemployed father.

"I took it personally and was concerned for Edgar," Schmidt said. "All I could think of doing was to emphasize that now he could go home and spend time with his new baby and wife. I bought him a present for the baby and told him it would work out for the best. We hugged, cried, and said good-bye."

After each game, Schmidt had to file reports to his bosses in Philadelphia. He would write detailed emails and leave lengthy voicemails. The administrative work took about 40 minutes per day. It was easier than his task on the field.

The Threshers started 4–14 and were in last place by late April. But Schmidt understood he would not be judged by the standings. He stressed fundamentals and preached about playing the game the right way.

"This job requires a lot of patience," he said after the early slump. "You work with a kid in the afternoon or talk to the team and stress a particular concept. Then that night, the situation comes up where that very thing you pointed out is forgotten or ignored. That's the hardest thing. But they play hard, show up early, and do whatever we ask. If they're short on ability, they make up for it with hustle and a good attitude."

It was a long summer for Schmidt and the Threshers. The team simply lacked the talent to compete against clubs with better prospects. Schmidt knew he could do more to win games, but sometimes he was hamstrung by the development process. Certain players had to pitch certain days, even if it meant removing someone from the game who was doing well.

That happened in a game against Daytona. Middle reliever Ryan Hutchison had retired six straight batters, but Schmidt was told earlier in the day that Francisco Butto had to pitch two innings because he had not thrown in three days. Butto came in, walked a few batters, and surrendered a long grand slam.

"I felt winning the game would have meant more to the team's development than pitching a couple innings did to Butto's, but that wasn't my call," Schmidt said. "And that sort of thing happened numerous times throughout the summer."

The Threshers finished 55–81 and Schmidt decided one year was enough. He enjoyed the experience, but had some differences with management in philosophy and pay structure.

"I always knew, without thinking much about it, that managers at the minor league level—and coaches at all levels—were treated like second-class citizens on the pay scale," Schmidt said. "But after spending seven months in their world as a manager in A-ball in 2004, I have developed a strong conviction that that's a dumb way to run a business."

Schmidt has a valid point. Minor league managers are the first to encounter top draft picks who are paid millions of dollars. These managers are required to not only teach players the fundamentals and help them develop their skills so the huge investment pays off, but to also serve as teachers and disciplinarians. Yet they earn approximately $30,000 for this important job.

"How many qualified men, with serious major league experience, would be candidates for long-term positions in player development if the salary fit the position?" Schmidt said. "Offer $250,000 to manage a Class A team and see how many former major league All-Stars call for an interview. Count me in! My point: in an industry in which the word *million* is thrown around like chump change, why don't the people who run it upgrade the compensation levels of the key individuals directly responsible for nurturing their most important asset?"

Schmidt's decision to step down after one season with the Threshers was not a big surprise to those who knew him.

"I think the Clearwater thing was something he just had to get out of his system and say, 'I can do it, I know I can do it, but I don't wanna do it. I don't wanna spend the time on it,'" Dallas Green said. "When you are a manager, whether it's the minor leagues or big leagues, it's so time-consuming and most players don't understand. Mentally, it just chews you up. Schmitty doesn't like that kind of stuff. He doesn't mind the physical work, but I think he did that to satisfy himself that he can do it and he can be successful at it and he probably could've been."

Less than a month after Schmidt resigned as Clearwater's manager, the Phillies fired Bowa. He had three winning seasons in four years, but failed to lead the Phillies into the playoffs. Schmidt did not agree with Bowa's dismissal, calling it a "raw deal." The bright side for him was that he thought he might be considered as a candidate to replace his former teammate in the Phillies' dugout.

Ed Wade interviewed eight men for the job. The list included former major league managers Jim Leyland, Don Baylor, Charlie Manuel, Grady Little, Buddy Bell, and Jim Fregosi. Pittsburgh Pirates third-base coach John Russell, a former first-round pick of the Phillies, and Atlanta Braves hitting coach Terry Pendleton also were interviewed. Once again, Schmidt was spurned by the Phillies.

"Sure, I was disappointed in not being considered for the Phillies job in 2004, even though I understood at the time why I wasn't," Schmidt said. "Their No. 1 priority was prior experience managing in the big leagues, and I had none."

Manuel, who led the Cleveland Indians to a division title in 2001, got the job, an unpopular pick in a city that longed for a champion and wanted Leyland, who won a World Series with the Marlins in 1997. Manuel was ridiculed for his accent—a thick Appalachian drawl—and his elocution. He was criticized heavily for his in-game strategy and was constantly second-guessed. But the thick-skinned Manuel ignored the naysayers and did his job. He finally won over the doubters by guiding the Phillies to a World Series championship in 2008 and a repeat appearance in 2009. Schmidt was one of his biggest supporters along the way.

"Charlie is one of the most honest, trustworthy, passionate baseball men I've ever met," Schmidt said. "He's a very secure individual, always keeps things in perspective, and never overreacts to the little issues that arise over the long season. Charlie is happy working anywhere in the game, and never changes. I've never heard him say a bad thing about another person."

Schmidt works on Manuel's staff in spring training, having returned to his role as a special hitting instructor with the Phillies. He gets his baseball fix now by spending a couple weeks in February talking hitting with guys like Ryan Howard, Chase Utley, and Jimmy Rollins. And, if the Phillies need a pep talk during the season, Schmidt is more than willing to provide it.

Schmidt reached out to Manuel and the team before a crucial series against the New York Mets in early September 2008. The Phillies had just lost two of three against the woeful Washington Nationals and trailed the first-place Mets by three games going into that series at Shea Stadium. Schmidt sent Manuel an email in which he encouraged the players and reminded them that they overcame New York's seven-game lead with 17 games left in 2007. Manuel printed it out and posted the message on the door of the clubhouse for players to see on their way to batting practice.

"One pitch, one at-bat, one play, one situation, think 'small' and 'big' things result, tough at-bats, lots of walks, stay up the middle with men on base, whatever it takes to 'keep the line moving' on offense, 27 outs on defense, the Mets know you're better than they are," Schmidt wrote. "They remember last year. You guys are never out of a game. Welcome the challenge that confronts you this weekend. You are the stars. Good luck. 20."

Manuel was not concerned about the Mets treating Schmidt's comments as bulletin-board material. After their historic collapse in '07, the Mets already had plenty of motivation.

"I have a lot of respect for Mike and I love talking baseball with him. It seems we're kind of on the same page when we talk," Manuel said. "I think that was him really sending us a message of how much he likes us and how much he's pulling for us to win. That's what I got in that message. I think our guys, especially the ones that were here last year and the veteran guys on our team, I think they know what we have to do, what's at stake. And I think we know how we're supposed to handle it. I think the entire message was very good. I think he was reminding them how good he thinks they are."

Perhaps the rallying cry from their former hero inspired the Phillies. Maybe it had no effect. No matter—the Phillies won two out of three from the Mets and went 14–5 the rest of the way to clinch their second straight NL East title. They cruised through the postseason, going 11–3 against the Milwaukee Brewers, Los Angeles

Dodgers, and Tampa Bay Rays to capture the second World Series title in franchise history.

Schmidt was most impressed by the team's resiliency throughout the season. He pointed to the series in New York as the turning point.

"They were three games out going into New York," he said. "They could have dumped the whole thing right then by losing the first game, allowing the Mets to have some momentum in that series. It could have gone to four games out, five games out. With 20 games to play, being five games out, it would have been a tough thing to overcome. If there ever was a turning point in their season during a championship year like that, it was that series in New York.

"They won the first two games, actually could have won the third. The rest is history. By resiliency, that's what I mean. Just at the time when you think that they're going to be affected by what's being written about them, how they're playing, how they're hitting, a lot of negatives are being thrown around Philadelphia, their resiliency surfaced and they went right into New York and took two out of three."

Schmidt writes more than just motivational emails in his spare time. He occasionally writes columns for *The Associated Press*. Schmidt has shared his thoughts on various baseball topics for AP since 2006. He has discussed the steroid controversy, Pete Rose's lifetime ban from baseball, instant replay, and the World Baseball Classic, among other subjects.

Here are excerpts from some of Schmidt's columns:

December 20, 2006

Headline: Mike Schmidt on Hall voting: More players deserve recognition

"As a member, I am always intrigued by the members' meetings in Cooperstown when we discuss the Veterans Committee ballot. Everyone has their guy, their crony, a past teammate they feel is being underrated. That's great that so many people, including the members, are concerned about the guys who just didn't make the grade—not to mention the real vote by the baseball writers, who now have to consider juiced balls, bats, and bodies.

"Having said that, ponder this question I posed at a recent meeting: doesn't a voter's opinion on a particular player have a great deal to do with how the voter himself perceives the Hall of Fame?"

July 5, 2007
Headline: Schmidt: Even as Bonds draws near, Aaron's reign will never really end

"Leave the steroid issue out of this. Maybe your eyes tell you one thing, but Barry has never failed a drug test. It's been guilt by association. He's had a long, amazingly productive career, a career that most likely will never be matched. He has been a five-tool player most of his career, combining speed, defense, hitting for average, and power. I lost count of his MVP Awards.

"I say appreciate it for what it is, the greatest career that spans two highly different generations. I say he is the greatest left-handed hitter of all time, maybe the greatest player—surely of our generation. And I'll bet that he is not that bad of a guy if you got to know him."

September 27, 2007
Headline: Schmidt: A-Rod needs to ease up as October pressure builds

"With all due respect to the great years by my friends George, Wade, and Brooks, the greatest year ever by a third baseman will very soon be owned by Alex Rodriguez. He'll eclipse my year in 1980 when we won the World Series, Brett's MVP and near-.400 year, and you can pick any one of several great years by Boggs and Robinson.

"My regular season of 48 home runs and 122 RBIs looks rather minuscule in comparison, but project that into today's environment and it would be similar. A-Rod winning a unanimous MVP is his next hurdle, and that should be no problem. The challenge ahead is his well-documented nemesis, as it was for me: the postseason."

October 24, 2007

Headline: Schmidt: Time for baseball to go to the replay...or is it?

"Oh, yes, the umpires will have to check their egos and understand, like football officials, they are human and sometimes get the play wrong. Even if replay and baseball get together someday soon, umpires will still be subject to critical calls at critical times. The amazing thing is they get it right 98 percent of the time. The issue is clearly that in today's sports megamoney environment, with so much at stake, should the human element be the final judge? Upon further review, the game stands as is!"

December 10, 2008

Headline: Schmidt: How about a one-and-done Hall election?

"I'd bet if you polled 100 'almost' Hall of Famers over the past 50 years, they'd agree that stringing them along for a number of years was worse than 'yes' or 'no' in their first year of eligibility. I know most baseball writers take their vote seriously. Imagine how serious they'd take it if it was 'yes' or 'no.' You're a Hall of Famer or you're not. No statement to make with a vote, no 'he's a second-ballot guy' or making him wait because he snubbed the press."

March 25, 2009

Headline: Schmidt: WBC was great, but what about its future?

"The three weeks on the road with Team USA offered an added dimension to my resume. If I may brag a little, I could coach third base for any big-league team. I really enjoyed that experience, but couldn't afford the job. At 60 years of age, being able to be on the field again, to feel like a small part of the formidable offensive attack, was invigorating. Going into the WBC, I was worried about screwing up, being self-conscious, losing concentration and, worst-case scenario, running Derek Jeter into a collision at home and costing the USA a championship.

"Not! I had all the moves. Sunflower seeds, bubble gum, and some dugout spitting was a carry-over from 30 years ago. I had the stances going, hands in back pockets, hands tucked in pants when cold, hands on knees, legs spread, it looks like you're into it and it's easier to avoid a line drive coming at you. I had the signs down, actually gave a couple real ones."

June 4, 2009

Headline: Schmidt: Who's voting for Manny in All-Star game?

"There are rumors that Manny Ramirez could be elected to start in the 2009 All-Star Game while serving a suspension for using a banned substance. I suppose this wasn't blatant 'steroid use'—you know, the 'needle' kind—but it did show some degree of ignorance and lack of respect for the game.

"After all, he had to know he would be tested. The message from fans must be that they don't care about a player's image or his moral fiber, they care only about what he can do between the lines. Fans are quick to forget, they've become tolerant, hardened, they're used to superstar athletes having issues. New ones seem to crop up every day."

July 30, 2009

Headline: Schmidt: Autograph craze is out of whack

"I'll be perfectly honest, I hate playing the cat-and-mouse game with collectors on the street. It was one of the reasons I retired early. Being targeted and stalked everywhere by people seeking a chicken-scratched slash on an inventory item is not fun. I'm not saying I'm a victim of paparazzi, but when airline luggage handlers wait for you in airports, your right to privacy is gone. When someone jumps out from behind a pillar in a parking lot as you're getting a rental car, you're being stalked. This isn't little Mike and his dad. These guys play games, they dress in costume, they hire little kids with sad faces and pretty girls in skimpy outfits, they make up stories, they lie, they even act polite, anything to get you to sign....

"Sure, there are some who say 'I'll never sell this' and maybe they are serious. But understand one thing—with my signature, sell it or not, that item increased in value from $10 to $100. Someday by someone it will be sold."

August 22, 2009

Headline: Schmidt on Pete Rose ban: Isn't 20 years enough?

"Pete bet on the Reds to win, never to lose. He never managed with the intention of not winning. Do you believe for one second the gambling underworld was tuned into Pete's betting habits? Pete never bet big or long enough to sway the gambling line. This has all been dressing to make it clear where gambling can lead. I'm not trying to say it's not serious—it is—but I'm asking you to compare its impact on the game to steroid use.

"Steroid players knowingly ingested chemicals that gave them an unfair advantage over clean players. Not only were they compromising the game's integrity, they were jeopardizing the long term for short-term financial gain, confusing baseball history. And, oh yes, some might've broken the law. Pete bet on his team to win and has been banished from baseball for life. Manny Ramirez, Alex Rodriguez, et al, bet that they would get bigger, stronger, and have a distinct advantage over everyone and that they wouldn't get caught. Which is worse? Does the penalty fit the crime?"

* * *

He entered the major leagues as Mike Schmidt, but thanks to Harry Kalas, he will forever be known to Phillies fans as Michael Jack Schmidt.

Kalas is the reason Schmidt's middle name became so popular. The Hall of Fame broadcaster called nearly every one of Schmidt's 548 career homers, often emphasizing his call with his smooth delivery: "Swing and a long drive. Watch that baby. Outta here. Home run Michael Jack Schmidt."

"Harry put the Jack in Michael Jack," Schmidt said a few days after Kalas died in April 2009. "He gave me this, I call it an endearing nickname, but it is my name. I was never called Michael Jack by my parents, ever. In fact, my middle name was hardly ever used until Harry Kalas labeled me. Everywhere I go now, people I've never met before in my life, they say, 'Nice to meet you, Michael Jack.' It's a cool thing. I'll forever see Harry's face now from here on out when I'm called Michael Jack. It's a warm thing. I appreciate it when people call me Michael Jack. It brings back a lot of memories for me. It's an endearing nickname."

Kalas was a legendary figure in Philadelphia who was respected and beloved by everyone. He passed away at age 73 in the broadcast booth in Washington before the Phillies played a game against the Nationals on April 13, 2009. Schmidt and Kalas were close friends and Phillies fans realized there was a special connection between them. Hours after Kalas died, fans began building a shrine around the statue of Schmidt that stands outside Citizens Bank Park. Someone left a small radio at the statue's feet. Several fans left baseballs, hats, pictures, and notes.

"It was very touching," Schmidt said. "I saved the pictures. I sent the photos to my mother and father. I'm honored that fans would think of my statue as a place where they can honor Harry's life.... Harry Kalas, if you look past Ben Franklin and William Penn, may have been the greatest person to grace the city of Philadelphia. As many lives as he affected, who would've had a bigger impact on the city? I can't think of anybody."

Schmidt was one of several speakers at a memorial service the Phillies held for Kalas at the ballpark on April 18. Thousands of fans, former and current players, friends, and family members filed into the stadium to bid farewell to Kalas, whose casket was placed behind home plate.

When it came time for Schmidt to address the crowd, Phillies broadcaster Tom McCarthy introduced him. "Many of you, about 25 years ago, something changed in the way you looked at a player. You knew their names, their first name, their last name. You might have even known their hometown," McCarthy said. "But it was a quarter of a century ago that you probably started to look up the middle names of all the players that wore a Phillies uniform. Nobody's middle name was made more famous or whose career was called so eloquently than Michael Jack Schmidt."

Fans cheered as Schmidt walked to the podium located inside the batter's box. On the 22nd anniversary of his 500th career home run, Schmidt delivered a moving eight-minute speech from his heart to eulogize his friend.

"Harry left us too soon, and with that came a jolt," Schmidt said. "We weren't prepared. We never got to retire his microphone, give him a retirement send-off night, or build a statue. Funny—he presided over all our special ceremonies, but never got one of his own. Most important, though, is Harry's legacy. It's a simple legacy, but on God's list, it ranks very near the top. It's not the voice that will ring our ears, or the 40 years of dedication to his work, or his passion for the game. It's that every day Harry was inspired to make people happy."

Schmidt talked about the way players viewed Kalas as one of them instead of a member of the media. He said Kalas would sit in the back of the plane on the team's charter flights and hold court with the veteran players. Before games, Kalas would walk through the clubhouse, offering words of encouragement or saying something to lift a player's spirits if needed.

"Heck, he even made me laugh before a game," said Schmidt, alluding to his stoic demeanor.

Schmidt walked off the field to a standing ovation. He connected with the fans at Kalas' memorial in a special way and earned praise for an impressive performance behind the microphone.

"That was one of his greatest moments," Dallas Green said. "I never heard him any better than he was at Harry's memorial. That was one of the greatest speeches and it came straight from the heart."

On a day filled with sadness, Mike Schmidt was at his finest. He comforted Phillies fans and the entire city of Philadelphia. The same man who used to be criticized for playing without emotion and for being "too cool" displayed a side of himself that fans rarely saw during his playing days, and they embraced him for showing it.

On that day, the people of Philadelphia got to see a sensitive, compassionate human being who mourned the loss of a great friend the same way they did. Mike Schmidt hit 548 home runs, won three MVP Awards, and owned a World Series ring. He was superhuman on the baseball diamond, but off the field he was just like the average fan.

Finally, Michael Jack Schmidt was one of them.

Acknowledgments

Many thanks to everyone who helped make this project a reality. A special thanks to those who took the time to grant me interviews, especially Dallas Green, Larry Bowa, and Juan Samuel. Thanks also to Ben Walker, Jack Scheuer, Larry Shenk, Chris Wheeler, Skip Clayton, and many others who allowed me to pick their brains. All the reporters and columnists who covered Mike Schmidt throughout his career for the *Philadelphia Inquirer*, the *Philadelphia Daily News*, and other media outlets were a tremendous resource. Thanks to Jayson Stark for his elegantly written foreword. Lastly, thank you to the crew at Triumph Books for giving me this opportunity: Scott Rowan, who made this happen, and Adam Motin, who made sure I was always on the right track.

Selected Bibliography

Schmidt, Mike. *Clearing the Bases*. New York: HarperCollins, 2006.

Schmidt, Mike. *Always On The Offense*. New York: Atheneum, 1982.

Kashatus C, William. *Mike Schmidt: Philadelphia's Hall of Fame Third Baseman*. North Carolina: McFarland & Company, 2000.

Jordan, David. *Pete Rose: A Biography*. Connecticut: Greenwood Publishing Group, 2004.

Kashatus C, William. *Almost a Dynasty: The Rise and Fall of the 1980 Phillies*. Pennsylvania: University of Pennsylvania Press, 2008.

Winegardner, Mark. *Prophet of the Sandlots*. New York: Prentice Hall Press, 1990.

Hochman, Stan. *Mike Schmidt: Baseball's King of Swing*. New York: Random House, 1983.

Croce, Pat. *I Feel Great*. Philadelphia: Running Press, 2000.

Westcott, Rich. *Tales from the Phillies Dugout*. Illinois: Sports Publishing L.L.C., 2003.

Bilovsky, Frank and Rich Westcott. *The Phillies Encyclopedia*. New York: Leisure Press, 1984.

Lewis, Allen. "Schmidt hits four homers." *Philadelphia Inquirer*, Sunday, April 18, 1976.

Freedman, Lewis. "Hero Schmidt: Amid storm, calm." *Philadelphia Inquirer*, Wednesday, October 22, 1980.

Stark, Jayson. "A staggering feat." *Philadelphia Inquirer*, Monday, April 20, 1987.

Silary, Ted. "Schmidt, Ashburn Wow 'Em." *Philadelphia Daily News*, Monday, July 31, 1995.

Bowen, Les. "The Mouth That Roared." *Philadelphia Daily News*, Tuesday, May 30, 1989.

Bernstein, Ralph. "Mike Schmidt-MVP." *The Associated Press*, Wednesday, November 19, 1986.

Hagen, Paul. "An Interview on the State of the Phillies and State of Baseball." *Philadelphia Daily News*, Tuesday, April 7, 1987.

Conlin, Bill. "The Run to 500." *Philadelphia Daily News*, Tuesday, April 7, 1987.

Robinson, Alan. "Phillies-Pirates." *The Associated Press*, Saturday, April 18, 1987.

Bernstein, Ralph. "Cubs-Phillies." *The Associated Press*, Tuesday, July 2, 1985.

Dolson, Frank. "A rookie struggle." *Philadelphia Inquirer*, Monday, April 20, 1987.

Searcy, Jay. "College years." *Philadelphia Inquirer*, Monday, April 20, 1987.

Searcy, Jay. "Back home in Ohio." *Philadelphia Inquirer*, Monday, April 20, 1987.

Searcy, Jay. "A baseball prodigy." *Philadelphia Inquirer*, Monday, April 20, 1987.

Juliano, Joe. "A season of scorn." *Philadelphia Inquirer*, Monday, April 20, 1987.

Hagen, Paul. "Schmidt Retires; Says His Skills Have Deteriorated." *Philadelphia Daily News*, Tuesday, May 30, 1989.

Ashburn, Rich. "No Sunday Silence." *Philadelphia Daily News*, Tuesday, May 30, 1989.

Hoffman, Rich. "He's Going Out with His Pride Intact." *Philadelphia Daily News*, Tuesday, May 30, 1989.

Hoffman, Rich. "A Future with Phillies Seems Uncertain." *Philadelphia Daily News*, Tuesday, May 30, 1989.

Cataldi, Angelo. "Phils Look for Their Leader and Find Only Their Star." *Philadelphia Inquirer*, Sunday, May 29, 1988.

Stark, Jayson. "A Smile After Months of Doubt." *Philadelphia Inquirer*, Thursday, December 8, 1988.

Dolson, Frank. "Schmidt's Last Stand?" *Philadelphia Inquirer*, Monday, April 3, 1989.

Weber, Dan. "Tony Lucadello's loyalty paid off." *Philadelphia Inquirer*, Thursday, June 1, 1989.

Didinger, Ray. "Schmidt Trying To Connect." *Philadelphia Daily News*, Wednesday, May 29, 1991.

O'Loughlin, Joe. "Mike Schmidt Interview." *Baseball Digest*. March 2001.

Walker, Ben. "Schmidt, Phils eager to extend relationship." *The Associated Press*, Wednesday, March 6, 2002.

Williams, Pete. "Hall of Famer Schmidt takes a minor step." *USA Today*, Tuesday, April 27, 2004.

Wulf, Steve. "In Philadelphia, They're The Wheeze Kids." *Sports Illustrated*, March 14, 1983.

Hagen, Paul. "Schmidt's retirement decision caught teammates by surprise." *Philadelphia Daily News*, Thursday, May 21, 2009.

Philadelphia Daily News. "What They're Saying." Tuesday, May 30, 1989.

www.cbssports.com.

www.baseballreference.com

About the Author

Rob Maaddi has covered Philadelphia sports for The Associated Press since 2000. He's covered the World Series, Super Bowl, NBA Finals, Stanley Cup Playoffs, and numerous major sporting events in the past decade. Maaddi graduated from Rutgers-Camden in 1996 and Temple University in 2002. He played college baseball, has coauthored three children's sports books, and hosted a weekly sports talk show on an ESPN radio affiliate. A lifelong Philadelphia-area resident, Maaddi currently resides in Sewell, New Jersey.